Books are to be returned on or before
the last date below.

LIBREX —

THE LANGUAGE OF FASHION & DESIGN
Creative, Multifarious, Global

THE LANGUAGE OF FASHION & DESIGN
Creative, Multifarious, Global

Edited by Helmut Merkel, Alexandra Hildebrandt, and Annett Koeman

reddot edition

THE LANGUAGE OF FASHION & DESIGN
CREATIVE, MULTIFARIOUS, GLOBAL

THE ONLY REVOLUTIONARY POWER IS
THE POWER OF HUMAN CREATIVITY.
JOSEPH BEUYS

ON THE VALUE OF CREATIVITY
WHAT WE CAN LEARN FROM DESIGNERS

By Thomas Middelhoff

It is the ideas of creative people that change society and business in equal measure. A group like Arcandor AG also lives off good ideas. Those who want to be successful in the long term and create value for their shareholders and stakeholders must constantly get to grips with new procedures and ways of thinking. This is also reflected in our slogan: "Committed to creating value." Creativity comes from the Latin word "creare," which means "to bring something new into being," to originate, to follow an inspiration. Something new comes into being when we consider what we do from constantly changing perspectives. That applies equally to innovative companies, which regard themselves as learning organizations. Such companies owe their success, above all, to committed, enthusiastic, and creative employees who take joy in their work. They inspire each other, make connections, and open up new horizons; they have the courage to try something new and in doing so are not frightened of making mistakes, as one cannot be had without the other – without risk there can be no opportunity.

It was Shakespeare who said, famously, that all the world's a stage. Applied to a company like Arcandor, this means that the employees are not just taking part in a good performance but are also being given an opportunity to see what is going on behind the scenes (of their company), the aim being to give them an insight into innovative activities. This is shown very clearly in the area of design, which exerts considerable influence on market positioning, product successes, and communication. Designers give their ideas a lasting form – sometimes they are also visionaries who have the courage to do what they believe in. In order to do this, they need to be assertive and have a keen sense for what will succeed in the market. This has everything to do with strength and nothing to do with weakness, since anyone who is able to seize an opportunity at the right moment, like fortune, is also capable of making a difference.

Norintra House of Fashion, our design center in Hong Kong, benefits from the close cooperation of designers, trend scouts, and suppliers from all over the world. Particularly through its cooperation with Li & Fung, one of the world's largest fashion houses and purchasing companies, Norintra is able to react to new trends very quickly. The design center's permanent staff come from countries such as China, Germany, and France. Norintra works with freelancers and partners from different cultural backgrounds throughout the world.

"Designers are a sort of mediator between their own ideas and the wishes of customers. They belong to a group of talented people who instinctively know that they need a special environment in order to develop fully."

Cultural diversity has become a competitive factor and is intended to foster creativity, innovation, and customer orientation. Different aesthetic concepts come together to create an interculturally crafted product. The Director of Norintra, Annett Koeman, sums it up thus: "The value added produced by cultural diversity improves problem solving and increases creativity, innovation, and customer care. And ultimately it creates a better working atmosphere, which in turn is a factor in economic success."

Designers are a sort of mediator between their own ideas and the wishes of customers. They belong to a group of talented people who instinctively know that they need a special environment in order to develop fully. They gravitate towards the urban jungle so they can be inspired by the latest developments. Their talent needs constant nourishment, otherwise it wanes over time. What are the characteristics of a talented designer, one who feels a constant urge to innovate? They include industry and endeavor, obsession, tenacity of thinking, doggedness in treading the beaten path, and openness to new experiences. These are crucial prerequisites for the design of products that are generally admired as creative or indeed brilliant. Materials, shapes, and colors from everywhere send out signals to their senses. These are the raw materials they work with. Designers put their souls, dreams, aspirations, and ideals into what is the understated product of their personality. They are constantly searching for freshness and originality. They know that the unknown always offers an extra dimension. Order and routine destroy creativity. Those who continue to think the way they have always thought will also get what they have always got – the same old ideas. Designers know that new ideas come about only through new impulses. And it is exactly this working style that is emphasized not only in our design center, but also throughout the Arcandor group. People who commit themselves and all their creative capacities to the company contribute to the creation of value added!

At Norintra, design teams work together closely in networks in order to provide quick, flexible, and efficient customer support in the development of new fashion creations. They are clever, creative, and talented. They are able to discern new trends emerging on the fashion horizon that others have not yet perceived. They mold their dreams in such a way that they can foresee trends and know what customers will want tomorrow.

This book is dedicated to them. They provide answers to the questions that preoccupy more or less every employee working for Arcandor AG: How do you stay open to inspiration? What is the greatest enemy of inspiration? How can you get an idea from nowhere? When is the best time to be creative? When is a product finished? When can nothing more be added? What does design have to do with the substance of a company? How are design and diversity linked? What makes a design center like Norintra "valuable"? Why does creativity require freedom? What characterizes products that are particularly successful in the market? Under what circumstances can economics and environmental awareness be fruitfully combined in the sphere of design?

Readers will pick out their own answers and find their own views echoed at various points. This is good, since it shows how much this topic concerns us all.

I hope the book provides inspiring and creative reading.

Yours
Dr. Thomas Middelhoff

FASHION IS NOT JUST ABOUT CLOTHES.
IT'S MORE ABOUT USING CLOTHES TO
COMMENT ON CLOTHES.
BARBARA VINKEN

DESIGNING AND CREATING VALUES DIALOG AND TOLERANCE BETWEEN DIFFERENT CULTURES IN AN INTER-NATIONAL CONTEXT

An introduction by Annett Koeman

This book – which is intended as a source and guide for business people and managers, fashion designers and consumers, scientists and artists – highlights not only the dialog and tolerance between different cultures in an international context, but also the economically and socially productive intercultural cooperation between executive boards and international subsidiaries. Creativity and diversity are revealed and explained using the example of six designers who work for the Norintra design center. Creative cities such as Hong Kong, characterized by an intensive service sector and a multitude of cultural achievements, act like a magnet for them.

Globalization is bringing people ever closer together, in business just as in everyday life. The problem: we all know too little about each other. The answers provided in this book give business and society key pointers for how to manage creativity and cultural diversity. The vision: to overcome invisible barriers in both business and everyday life. The aim of this book is to identify new ways of increasing company value, based on the example of the designers who work for Norintra. We need to ask questions such as: Why is it important to break with old conventions in order to create something innovative? How can we find new ideas? Why is potential better than experience? What can a manager learn from a designer? Why is quality better than quantity? What does it mean to create fashion? Why can no area of social life escape fashion? What goes into making a designer's style? What do they want and what can they achieve? Why do their designs appeal to us? – The focus here is on the designers' personal experiences and individual points of view. They all have one thing in common: they are "genuine" in the sense conveyed by Marion Gräfin Dönhoff, because they "follow their own standards and their intuition."

I hope the book inspires you.

Yours
Annett Koeman

THE ONLY THING WE NEED TO KNOW
ABOUT A PERSON IS WHETHER
OR NOT THAT PERSON MAKES OUR
THOUGHTS FRUITFUL.
ROBERT MUSIL

TO BE CREATIVE IS TO BE HUMAN CREATIVITY AS THE FUTURE CAPITAL OF A COMPANY

An interview with Emmanuel Siregar

Why does a company constantly need to mobilize new modes of thought and action among its employees if it really wants to sustain its success?

A company that wants to sustain its success will always be compared with other companies, because success is the positive outcome of a comparison. The more clearly we recognize and accept this connection, the easier it will be for our employees to understand it too. Every single manager in our company, every employee, every team, every group is compared with managers, employees, departments, teams, and groups in other companies.

Our task is, therefore, to create a working environment in which our employees can be successful, are able to use their creativity to achieve their goals, and are allowed to try out new modes of thought and action. I would like to stress here that the company's executive board is not actually able to mobilize new modes of thought and action among employees. All it can do is create an environment in which this can happen. Creativity and the potential for development are not things that can be delegated; they are the responsibility and freedom of the individual.

A design center such as Norintra in Hong Kong lives on the creativity of its employees. What do you regard as the essence of creativity? And what makes it the company's future capital?

When I read the article about Angel Wong, what moved me was that she sees her creativity as an independent viewpoint from deep within her. She's right: creativity is all about making and communicating. Creativity is a talent, a gift that I have been given initially without having earned or paid for it. Being able to communicate my creativity is, therefore, also a gift to other people, again not earned or paid for – after all, that's what a gift is.

So I don't see creativity as the starting point in a process chain that has to be sucked dry, but rather as the living heartbeat of human existence and thus of human activity and work. To be creative is to be human, because the essence of a human being lies in being able to leave one's mark and give oneself. A company's future capital is the goal-driven and intelligent harnessing of creativity, of creative people.

Why can creativity be a "value" in a company, but never an "agenda"?

Creativity as the ability to think, communicate, and achieve productively is not an agenda but is rather the inherent spirit of the agenda. Creativity needs the freedom of design and can be successful and achieve its aims only in this dynamic environment. However, once mobilized, creativity can certainly lead to standard processes being established.

The Arcandor motto, "Committed to creating value," makes the connection between creativity and value particularly clear. People create value. Agendas can, in turn, result from this creative work.

Why will creativity dominate the labor markets of the future?

We live in an era in which products, goods, and services are far more comparable than they were 10 or 20 years ago. Things that will require a great deal of creativity and intelligence on the part of the company and its employees will increasingly constitute the differences thrown up by the comparison, generated by the rivalry. A successful, intelligent approach is marked by swift reactions and creativity. That will be the key to success in the future.

What connects innovative people and innovative companies, and what promotes a culture of innovation?

Innovation means renewal. A culture of renewal can result only from creative approaches and impetus. Innovative people, therefore, belong in innovative companies. If we look at a company's structure not as the sum of its workforce but – to use a biblical image – as a whole body, we could say the executive board is the head, sales would be the legs, purchasing the hands, the public relations department the mouth, and controlling the brain. All the cells have the same DNA; they're identical to the company.

If we want to promote a culture of innovation in our company, we need innovative people with the same innovative gene for the body of this company. And we position innovative people where they can live out and successfully use their innovative force, for themselves and for the company. This requires a deft touch in personnel acquisition and in the positioning of new employees.

Designers who feel the urge for renewal act as a kind of mediator between their own ideas and the wishes of the customer. What can employees at Karstadt Warenhaus learn for their day-to-day work from a designer who works for Norintra in Hong Kong?

I like the idea of a mediator. Our employees can learn a great deal for their day-to-day work from a designer who works for Norintra in Hong Kong, as they themselves are, after all, mediators between the company and our customers out in the field. Any marketing concept, any innovative approach from the head office will not be well received by customers if our employees in the field are not in a position to communicate this content effectively. But I can communicate content only if it has already convinced me, that is, if I am not merely a dispensable bearer of a message but in the best sense a representative of my company: an ambassador, or mediator of this message. That's what I find so fascinating about designers. They communicate something that comes from inside – and Angel Wong reveals her soul through her work.

A truly customer-oriented salesperson in a department store should communicate to a customer from deep within, should explain our marketing strategy, our products, our services – because the salesperson is convinced by them, and believes in them so much that they come from within. In their dealings with customers, salespeople are sales designers, messengers of a multilayered communication that our customers receive with enthusiasm because they themselves are convinced by the salespeople, are infected by their enthusiasm. Sales employees are communication designers.

Creativity researcher Dean Keith Simonton once said that in order to get good grades in school you usually have to largely adopt the conventional image of the world and humanity. So basically, those who fit in best get good grades. Often, those who are talented and intelligent get worse grades because they prefer to concentrate on other things that they are more interested in. What is the importance of resumes or school and university certificates when selecting potential candidates? How do you identify talented and creative employees? What do you look out for when interviewing a candidate?

Naturally, all of us in HR will look at resumes, school and university certificates, references from previous employers, and so on. Form and content belong together. But I'm more likely to recognize the personal potential of candidates by reading between the lines. So the candidate's favorite subject at school is more important than the resulting grade, even if it does indicate a tendency. Involvement in a sports club or with Amnesty International says more than a preformulated letter of reference does. The way candidates express themselves and listen is more important than a document about a rhetoric seminar or a presentation that they might have attended.

However, I would not generally equate good grades with the ability to fit in. To achieve good grades, particularly across the board, you need to be very goal-driven, hardworking and, above all, creative. In this respect I am more inclined to believe that those who fit in get quite mediocre grades, while those who do not fit in sometimes get an F, and sometimes an A. Mediocrity gives rise to mediocrity, high performance does not mean fitting in, it means creative commitment far beyond the norm.

Why is it important to allow for creative risks in a company and to stand by a culture of mistakes? After all, it has been proven that the most creative people are generally those who have experienced the most failures. People who aren't prepared to take a risk can't make mistakes either.

That's true; mistakes are part and parcel of it. However, we can't simply sit back and accept mistakes. I don't like the idea of a culture of mistakes. I would rather talk of a culture of correcting or avoiding mistakes. The creative aspect of mistakes is the constructive revision that comes after them, rather than the simple acceptance of mistakes or errors as part of a process. For me, the important thing in a culture of dealing with mistakes is that these mistakes are analyzed and recognized as such and – this is the decisive factor – are tackled together. A precise analysis and look back must be quickly followed by joint commitment. On the basis of this joint agreement, it is then necessary to draw up a list of measures to correct the mistakes, and to start implementing these measures so as to ensure that we learn lessons from these mistakes as a way of contributing to future success.

I therefore believe that we must really move from a culture of covering up mistakes to a culture of dealing with mistakes, which – put in positive terms – must become a creative culture of mutual correction. We must learn to correct each other constructively. That's why it is important for an individual to be appreciated and not to be associated with a mistake. I therefore believe that we – and this also has to do with creating value – need to arrive at a culture of mutual appreciation, which starts with the customer, includes the workforce in its entirety, and must become a principle of culture right through to the company management and executives.

Is failure the key to innovation?

Failure itself is not the key to innovation but could well be the way to achieve it. It's the way we deal with failure that holds the key to innovation. How to deal with failure can be learned. It's related to the acceptance of oneself and of others, and is therefore an existential rather than a deliberate process. Ultimately, this road from failure to innovation is a similar procedure to the one I tried to describe in connection with creativity: the ability to move from failure to innovation is more a gift than a deliberate act. It's a passion in the truest sense of the word and in the way passion is used in the context of Christian religions, the way from failure and defeat to a new existential point of view.

Ethically sound business (corporate social responsibility) is the response to increasingly critical consumers. On this subject, Peter

A creative culture of mutual feedback is promoted at team meetings.

"Innovation means renewal. A culture of renewal can result only from creative approaches and impetus. Innovative people, there-fore, belong in innovative companies."

Creativity is a talent, a gift that nonetheless requires constant input.

Wolf, chairman of the management board of Karstadt Warenhaus GmbH and member of the managing board of Arcandor AG, said: "Customers 'feel' fashion in the truest sense of the word. The more carefully a piece of clothing is produced from the outset and the more reliably it is checked for possible residues, the more comfortable you will feel wearing it. However, the items of clothing must also be fashionable. Customers who buy one of these products not only have a comfortable item of clothing, they can also rest assured that they have made an active ecological contribution." Can you imagine combining the subject of ethical fashion, that is to say, the consequence of the organic food boom, with a personnel development program?

Peter Wolf is not simply talking about ecology, he is primarily talking about product excellence, and within product excellence he determines the ethical background of an ecological approach. Personnel development will also develop in a similar vein, derived from Peter Wolf's approach. We first need operational excellence in relation to the product, operational excellence in relation to management processes, operational excellence in relation to personnel development, and within this claim of operational excellence, we also need to incorporate the ethical standard of customer orientation, employee advancement, and other ethical standards that we as a group formulate.

The philosophy behind Peter Wolf's words is wide-ranging. It includes the complete value chain from marketing, purchasing, and sales right through to the customer. And it does not define the customer as the final element, and therefore sales as the point at which the purchasing manager hands over, but rather sees the customer as the starting point for all thought, action, and management.

The customer is the basis on which we develop the product range, the division of floor space, the presentation for the customers, the advertising that draws the customers into our Karstadt stores. The customer is the basis on which we also define our products, follow or set trends, and conduct our purchasing activities, so that the customer receives excellent products.

The customer is also the basis for our personnel development measures, because employees are there to help customers. Our company's philosophy is "Committed to creating value": together, we want to create innovative value so that motivated managers are able to develop motivated employees who serve and advise enthusiastic customers. Only enthusiastic managers can inspire enthusiasm in employees. Only enthusiastic employees can inspire enthusiasm in customers. Only products worthy of enthusiasm can persuade customers to shop at Karstadt. That means: we want to live customer orientation.

WHY CAN'T I TRY ON DIFFERENT
LIVES LIKE CLOTHES, TO SEE WHAT
SUITS ME BEST?
SYLVIA PLATH

CREATIVE, MULTIFARIOUS, GLOBAL CULTURAL DIVERSITY IS BECOMING A COMPETITIVE FACTOR IN A GLOBALIZED WORLD

An interview with Annett Koeman

What does Norintra House of Fashion stand for? And what makes it special?

Norintra is an important point of contact between designers and buyers, between theory and practice, between communication, the public, and business. The name stands for awakening, creativity, change, and cultural diversity – the decisive competitive factors of Norintra House of Fashion.

What do you regard as your most important task?

As head of the design center I make sure that we have the right environment for creative people to express themselves. I also provide impetus for current trends, supply information, and am the link to our stakeholders. To enable my employees to contribute and express themselves, we at Norintra provide just the right framework for their creativity, which is necessary to achieve the best possible results. At the same time I manage them in such a way that they do not directly perceive it and can concentrate fully on their work. After all, creative people are generally more sensitive and receptive to external influences than others are, and management should be sure to take this into account, because sensitivity is precisely the strength that makes their products so exceptional.

How do you communicate the latest trends and developments, both within the company and to the outside world?

Anyone who is interested can receive regular updates – for example, fashion reports at the start of the season, the monthly trend and store check reports, and information on the latest developments in production. We are also involved in cross-group communication projects that promote dialogue and tolerance between cultures at international level and support the economic and socially productive intercultural cooperation between management and subsidiaries. The Culture Counts project, for example, illustrates hot spots of cultural diversity in the company in a publication by the corporate group. We are involved in this. The people we work with come from the United Kingdom, France, Japan, the United States, for example – we have a global network. Despite cultural differences, we must all work together closely – across different time zones – and this shows on a small scale how people are becoming closer as a result of globalization. This is the starting point for Culture Counts: How do people live and work around the world? The project's vision is to overcome the invisible barriers in business and life. But it is also primarily about cultural diversity, and makes a contribution to the dialogue between cultures that is also taking place at this very moment at Norintra.

Your intention at Norintra is to develop fashionable styles, but at the same time to consider how this is done – so it's about a sustainable value chain?

Yes, we want to show that Fair Fashion in the industry is a market to be taken seriously, that it can be cool, sexy, and trendy but not empty. It's about the "depth" that exists on the surface. As I mentioned, we are currently working on an ecological collection. But our concept will only catch on when ecological is sexy and the styling speaks to the customer. Good design and a social conscience can be combined very effectively – as the success of well-known brands has shown.

In this age of bargain-hunting, isn't it difficult to get this message across?

It is undoubtedly a problem when the main thing on so many consumers' minds is cheap goods. Buyers must relearn that quality comes at a price. Everyone has a moral responsibility to think about the conditions under which textiles are produced. It is natural for us to put this across in our numerous communication campaigns. The volume of positive feedback shows us that we are on the right path.

Numerous factors are involved in the design of a textile: economy, comfort, brand identity, and ecology. Which areas pose the greatest difficulties for your designers, because they require the greatest concessions?

In recent months the development of materials has been progressing very well. For example, materials that previously felt stiff and scratchy are now soft and flowing. Up until recently this was a problem, because you cannot treat organic cotton materials with chemicals. The industry has now returned to a few old tried-and-tested methods: for example, washing jeans with pumice stone. This gives us exactly the right washed look we need for a fashionable collection.

It's impossible to speak objectively about design – so much comes down to emotional decisions. Can you nevertheless explain what, in your opinion, makes a good design?

Good design combines global and local aspects; for me, it is a combination of look, comfort, and ease of care. If I buy something today, I want to look great, I want to feel comfortable when I wear it, and I want to still like it after I've washed it.

Does "beauty" play a role as an emotional quality in your design deliberations?

We can draw parallels with relationships here. Most people first notice appearances, or "beauty." But after a while that is not enough if other qualities are missing. A relationship depends on whether you have shared interests and values, in other words, a lasting quality in your partnership. This is also one element of a successful brand. You need to have a deep trust in the quality of the products and be able to guarantee this to consumers.

What makes a good designer?

Designers are people who push the boundaries, because they must be prepared to fight hard for the best solution with their partners in development and production. Collaboration is characterized by respect and enthusiasm. Designers should have visions and the courage to pursue their beliefs. But as visionaries, they should also be able to fight for their ideas and concepts. They must be able to determine the right strategy at the right moment. Even though design is a very personal matter, they must be good communicators and networkers. And they need to be assertive. It is not enough to want to realize their ideas in isolation – the products must suit the brand and the target group.

How does Norintra find good designers? How do you keep them at the design center?

That's a major challenge for our personnel department. However, many employees come on recommendation. If we have a designer from the United Kingdom, for example, we are already known in the design circles there. And our good contacts with universities also help us to attract new designers. We encourage employee development through specific seminars (for example, fabric courses, international trend courses and shows), but also with training in the area of language. One thing our employees really value is their involvement in cross-group projects, which give them a broader perspective for their work. Designers with their own distinctive hallmark who are also interested in developing their own collection are supported in their efforts, not hindered. This way they can develop their collection for the company.

Talent brings with it the urge for renewal. Companies should therefore find out more about talent and think about how to recognize and promote it. What does Norintra do to allow its designers' talent to be developed in the best possible way?

They work in an attractive environment with media stimulation such as Fashion TV and MTV, magazines or store checks in the fashion capitals of the world. They visit major art and fashion exhibitions, see the latest movies – usually in small groups to make sure that they can share their thoughts and work through them straightaway. We offer regular internal training and information on different topics – for example, new developments in materials and information and monitoring of upcoming designers. We have also just launched a partnership for design with a UK university. Students are offered placements with us: they work with our designers and product developers directly on the collections and learn how designs are produced. As a result, they gain important experience for their later professional lives – and with any luck the most talented will return to us after they graduate.

To what extent are the designers' values and creative approaches taken into consideration at Norintra? Do they have the opportunity to resist temporary fashions and contribute their own style and also take risks when creating their prototypes?

We talk to every brand manager in Germany about how many new, as yet untested trends they want to have in their collection. A certain number is essential so that fashion, individuality, and creativity can show their true colors.

If designers don't feel anything for the things they design, can they inspire passion for them in other people?

No. If you have no emotion you have no passion and thus no creativity. Our designers – each and every one of them – puts their life blood into their projects. What they feel for their designs is obvious at the very latest when they have to create the end products with the product developers, or if comments from management mean that changes are needed. Those aren't always the nicest situations, because every detail in the design is fought over. Design is a very personal matter – which does not mean that every designer has to love or want to wear every individual piece. What it does mean, though, is that the designers establish a strong connection during the design process, one that involves their heart and soul. Good designers lose themselves in their creative work, much like artists.

Can the designers expect a quick assessment of their designs from management?

In the handoff phase we have meetings practically every day. The division managers for design and product development need to plan their working days and business trips carefully to make sure that nothing slows down the process. We make sure that there is always a manager available to give approval.

Does feedback from employees and customers – their ideas and suggestions – influence product development?

Designers and consumers have one thing in common: sensitivity. It has everything to do with courage and nothing to do with weakness. It strengthens everyone who possesses it. Only sensitive people are receptive. And if you are receptive, you are able to change things. So the answer is most definitely "Yes."

Your team, which consists of international designers and trend scouts, is always on the lookout for the latest trends. How often do you meet to discuss the latest trends, fashion styles, materials, and technologies?

We meet regularly, at least once a week or as soon as there is something new to discuss – for example, if someone brings out a new collection with groundbreaking pieces. In future, we want to be the ones with the groundbreaking pieces.

How do you fill in the time until the next season's products?

The time when there were two seasons (summer/winter) is long gone. We work from month to month and can thus no longer talk of seasons as such, because the seasons flow into each other – from spring to summer, summer to fall, fall to winter... And then there are the special themes (Christmas, Easter, holidays). There are no gaps in the year where we don't have to design anything.

In the 17th century, fashion was the goddess of appearance, a kind of madness that no one could escape, the queen of social life. What, in your opinion, is the point of fashion in the 21st century?

We want to give our customers the opportunity to express themselves, to change and reveal their own identity. Fashion is a clear statement – for or against something. At the moment we can see this very clearly in the social debate about green glamour and ethical fashion. The subject is very close to my heart too. The transition from a niche subject to the mainstream is something we can neither ignore nor stop in its tracks. Like the cars that will probably run without petrol in the next century, we in the fashion

A special form of sustainability in the design center: retaining employees by means of training.

world are also facing an enormous challenge for the future: to produce ecological and fair clothing that reflects the taste of the time. It's about changing the world through small steps in your own immediate environment. Once we have got the first few miles behind us, the rest of the "global marathon" will be far easier.

Fashion is an important seismograph of general developments in the area of design. The art of reading clothing fashion fascinated Walter Benjamin in his Arcades Project, produced between 1927 and 1940: "Each season brings, in its newest creations, various secret signals of things to come." What does this statement mean to you?

I would like to answer with a second quote, from Oleg Cassini: "Fashion anticipates, and elegance is a state of mind ... a mirror of the time in which we live, a translation of the future, and should never be static." Both speak of the connection and changes of our times, which are reflected in our clothing. If you look back in fashion, it indicates the state of the world's population (and economy). A time of "excess" and extremes is always followed by a "hangover" – a period of minimalism and a focus on the basics.

You once said that Zeitgeist in fashion is most clearly demonstrated…

The determining factors associated with Zeitgeist include personality and character or individuality. You can see this very clearly in the emergence of the new, trendy ecological labels. There are retailers who pay celebrities to advertise fair fashion, which creates a certain amount of hype. As a result, it has also become fashionable to do something for the environment and to demonstrate one's own responsibility by buying certain products. Customer awareness will continue to grow in the future. People wearing an ecological label are demonstrating that they belong to a certain group, and that they see themselves as part of a greater whole. Lifestyle and behavior are inseparably tied to each other here.

Do you intend to show your prototypes in traveling exhibitions in high-class department stores around the world?

Not the prototypes – but you can see the products that result from them in the Karstadt stores or on the pages of one of the many catalogues. But we do go on tour with various limited editions, such as the Couture Evening Collection and our Fair Fashion Collection. For example, the eveningwear collection by our designer Angel Wong was shown exclusively at the awards for the German Culture Prize in September 2007 in Berlin.

Examining a style – taking it apart, so to speak – also means putting together things that appear mutually exclusive. Masters of style show that it is possible to walk the line between the present, past, and future. Why does style last, while fashions fade?

Style is the expression of an attitude that extends across different areas of life – one of these areas is clothes. Style is related to a sense of quality and the will to be individual. The fascinating thing about style is that it exists in the present, past, and future. The present relates to the current moment, which ensures that the clothes don't look outdated. The past points to timeless basics. These classics show that artistic quality cannot be reduced to mere novelty value. The winners of the future point to the avant-garde.

A while ago, the CEO of Hess Natur, Wolf Lüdge, said that the famous slogan "Geiz ist geil" (Cheap is cool) should be replaced by "Responsibility is sexy." Will ecological labels play a role at Norintra in the future?

Most definitely! Green chic can already be found on the catwalks of Paris and Milan. That shows that the times when ecological clothing was boring and shapeless are long gone. We need to move with this development because otherwise it will overtake us. We are already working on a sexy feminine collection in the fall. We want people to buy the commercial collection because they like the design – the fact that it's ecological is just the icing on the cake. We will be building on this – the combination of fair trade and fashionable style will play an important role for us in the future. Fashion is also an extension of one's own point of view, as the current ecological boom in all areas of life shows.

Why are you involved in the MADE-BY initiative?

MADE-BY makes clothes under fair working conditions and with minimum damage to the environment. This concept perfectly matches our own approach. It includes working together with suppliers from the Chinese market. Previously, most organic labels were produced in Peru, Turkey or Africa. We are in Hong Kong, close to the Chinese market, and therefore it is very important to us to push this here together with Chinese suppliers. Organic fabrics are already available on the market. We want to

As the head of the design center, Annett Koeman (center) ensures that the right framework is in place for creativity.

work up to fair trade by next year together with the suppliers and the MADE-BY organization.

How can you tell whether clothes come from MADE-BY?

By the blue button or a label picturing a blue button. This guarantees that the clothes were produced with respect towards people and the environment. The affiliated fashion brand sews a MADE-BY label into the clothes and this label contains a code, which you can enter on the check-it-out website (www.made-by.org). Here, you can display a picture of the factory and read an interview with the person who sat at the sewing machine or loom.

What does Norintra's claim "Creation of sustainable values" mean to you?

The claim in itself means nothing. People don't come to Norintra because of a claim. They – like our designers – must live the claim, be the claim. That is the best indication that the message has been understood and internalized.

EACH MATERIAL IS WORTH ONLY
WHAT WE MAKE OF IT.
LUDWIG MIES VAN DER ROHE

WORD AND DEED
LASTING COMMUNICATION USING
THE EXAMPLE OF NORINTRA

By Alexandra Hildebrandt

I. "To dress up is attractive: to let oneself be dressed up is sad."
Coco Chanel

For the commercial success of a product, communication – as a means of "dressing up" a particular message – is at least just as important as the manufacturing process itself. The values and feelings that the designers in this book talk about are also expressed in lasting communication; here, too, what matters is quality, attention to detail, and credibility. Similarly, social systems arise only through communication. WHAT is communicated is important, but in my opinion, HOW something is communicated is of even greater importance. This is one thing that communication has in common with fashion: it is (to quote Coco Chanel once again) "always a reflection of its own time, but we forget this if it is stupid."

Those who simply talk around the deed instead of actually doing it will ultimately not have much to "do" as they lack the substance that is absolutely essential in order to drive something forward. The more frequently they get to grips with a task, make decisions, and "do," the more new things and niches they create – and this is necessary when it comes to creating meaning. Good people in the fashion and communication industry do not wait until someone tells them what to do, they actively contribute to the company and create for themselves the position needed to carry through their ideas – regardless of all resistance. They don't ask about job descriptions, but rather see it as a challenge and a stroke of luck to be able to work from a clean slate.

Discoverers (and they have this in common with innovative designers) do not like to follow travel guides or detailed instructions, they simply prefer a map – they value information, but do not want to be guided through certain areas by so-called experts. Package tourists are convinced they know it all because they have visited and photographed famous sights. But this is not enough if you really want to see.

The situation is similar in the CSR sector: a basic knowledge is needed, but it is then necessary for you to seek out the locations and the people with whom you can undertake the project journey. For me, Norintra House of Fashion is a part of all this. The thing that drives us forward is something like a shared harmony. Our key areas are held together by project managers who always also give of themselves and make the overall results their own personal crusade. And that's the way it should be, because if heart and individuality are not part of what goes into the work, it can have no soul. And that can then be seen in the end result.

The content is what matters, and if the content is right, the "material" complies of its own accord. The added value of Norintra's

Understandable and tangible communication: with the "Cube," Norintra has developed a magic cube that communicates core statements on its different fold-out sides.

activities and products cannot simply be seen in a particular collection, for example, but also "in between." So the Norintra press kit is not a medium to be used temporarily, but is rather a medium that has been finely tuned to the overall communication targets, including those of Arcandor. The head of the design center, Annett Koeman, was therefore looking for an unusual and innovative medium to represent the value chain in detail. The result is a complex cube, a type of fold-out Rubik's Cube, whose various interchangeable surfaces communicate key statements from and about Norintra. At the same time, it shows how the effects of globalization are changing our world. This interplay goes right through the cube. There are always sides that are turned away, that you can't see. The task for the developers was to link 48 individual surfaces with one another in a complex way and to develop a script in the unfolding of the cube. There are four phases in which a story is told – and authentic communication also lives on stories.

As many customers are not design experts themselves, it is necessary to compensate for this in communication. And one of this book's key concerns is, therefore, to let design "speak" and to give a voice to those who are looking for the maximum possible concordance between their own aspiration for style and life in general.

II. "A great fashion designer thinks about the future even more than a great statesman. A designer's genius lies in the fact that he must design summer clothes in the winter, and vice versa. While his customers are sunbathing in the scorching heat, he is thinking of ice and frost." Coco Chanel

Fashion designers who want to find their foothold amid instability weave and are woven, spin and are spun, are dreamers and visionaries who contrast a fragmented life with the creation of something whole. They cross the boundary between reality and imagination, are obsessed with completion, relentlessly perfecting the world. If they tear it up in the morning, they will be sewing it back together in the evening. The beginning is the material of which their dreams are made. This is where they are at home and safe. For them, fashion is an expression of deep-seated feelings and longings. Materials, forms, and colors send signals to their senses from everywhere, and from this they shape their material. Everything that enters their life they draw into their life. "Genius, too, does nothing except learn first how to lay bricks, then how to build, except continually search for material and continually form itself around it," as Friedrich Nietzsche wrote.

In the interviews featured here, the designers show themselves as they are: creative people identical only to themselves. They make fashion for people who do not (need to) invent themselves but rather find what corresponds to them in the world of fashion. And that, too, is authentic communication.

"Fashion designers who want to find their foothold amid instability weave and are woven, spin and are spun, are dreamers and visionaries who contrast a fragmented life with the creation of something whole."

LANGUAGE IS NOT WHAT WE USE TO
DESCRIBE SOMETHING, BUT WHAT WE
USE TO THINK WITH.
PETER BICHSEL

The following chapter presents interviews with six young designers who work for the Norintra design center in Hong Kong. They give insights into their ideas on fashion, and explain where they get their inspiration from and how they manage to be creative again and again. The chapter concludes with a photo series showing the eveningwear collection of the designer Angel Wong Pui Shan.

ADAMS CHEUNG WAN-HO
A FASHION PHILOSOPHY IS A
LIVE EXPERIENCE

An interview with the designer

"A designer's most important tool is openness", according to Adams Cheung Wan-ho, who likes being exposed to a wide range of cultural and social influences in order to find continuing inspiration. For a designer, power of observation and sensitivity are the source of all creativity. Nevertheless, a designer also needs the tools of the trade. Adams says, "Every designer should have good visualization skills in order to be able to communicate ideas to others." Adams himself acquired a broad skill base in the field, initially studying Visual Communication and then Fashion Design at the Hong Kong Polytechnic University. He gained his first practical work experience in London, as an intern at the studios of the British fashion designer Jessica Ogden. After completing his studies, he worked as a fashion designer for the labels Kitterick, Antinori, and Noir, designing both ladies' and men's clothing.

43

Designers have to have good visualization skills in order to be able to communicate ideas to others and make their models a reality.

What does creating fashion mean to you? Being torn between two completely different elements: calmness and stress, stimulation and inner composure …

There are so many creative designers, for example, Hussein Chalayan, Comme des Garçons, Raf Simons, Viktor & Rolf. These are just some of my favorite designers, but in my view they are somewhat out of touch with reality, because the true challenge of a designer is to try to maintain and live out his creativity in the face of harsh reality – namely, commercial success.

Wolfgang Joop is firmly convinced that a fashion designer must have a feeling heart and eyes that have seen something of life. Do you share his view?

We designers are, of course, much more sensitive and empathetic than others. This enables us to analyze things in detail so as to integrate them into our work. If we want to be successful in our industry, this particular ability is an absolute must.

Is your fashion philosophy based on the cut?

A fashion philosophy is a living experience which changes to the extent that we ourselves change. The stages of development of a certain style that designers experience can, at first, be compared to the wind: we can feel it but we can't see it (yet).

Why should a fashion designer always be the harshest critic of his own ideas? To prevent him from becoming a slave of his first good idea?

The first design idea is like a seed which will one day develop into a fully-grown tree. I personally have never been a slave of my previous ideas. Ideally, a good designer should never run out of ideas, either.

What makes a creator of fashion an innovative designer?

Talent is, of course, the most important factor. In order to set trends and be innovative in the industry, a designer must also have extensive cultural knowledge, for example, in the fields of music, film, and art. He should also have a personal vision, even if it isn't overly spectacular, as well as an individual view of his designs and a certain feeling for things, a subtle sensitivity, and, of course, the ability to closely observe his environment. As couturiers, we have to know what's going on around us.

Do you consider yourself a kind of mediator between your own ideas and the customers' wishes and demands?

That really depends on the level of design we are talking about. When it comes to the mass market, I have to admit that designers are a kind of "customer service department" – which leaves very little space for "personal creativity."

If it's the market that determines the image of a brand and the success of individual products, what role can you as a designer play in this process?

It's because the market determines everything that it's so important to enhance the quality of design by adding a personal note. If a designer does not come up with new ideas, customers cannot take pleasure in a product's new attractiveness or appeal, and this can result in the loss of customers. When it comes to a fashion brand, the emphasis is always on novelties, but another task of the designer is more important, and that is to retain the advantages already gained.

Karl Lagerfeld once said that he wanted to deal with everyday problems as little as possible: "I'm an absolute egoist. My motto has always been: I'm the linchpin of everything that happens around me. To hell with everyone else." What do you think of this statement?

I wish I could say the same! But in reality, an egoistic, self-serving designer will soon find himself on the sidelines. The fashion industry is a very small circle, and a generally accepted professional etiquette is absolutely imperative, and has to be adhered to. A designer shouldn't live in his own small world, designed according to his own needs and wants; much rather, he should integrate his constantly changing environment into his work. Because that's the only place where the origin of creativity can be found.

Isn't designing like a trip into the unknown, with the designer uncertain whether he'll ever arrive at his destination because the travel route is constantly changing?

This particular unknown territory is exactly what makes my work so exciting. I draw my inspiration from things and elements that hardly anyone dares to change. Just imagine someone going to a business meeting wearing flip-flops: wouldn't that be cool? Wouldn't it be an act of genius if I were to design flip-flops which would optimally suit this strict and serious setting?

What is more important to you: the process (the journey) or the product (the arrival)?

The process means very much to me because it amounts to learning. That's our daily reward.

Why is designing so important to you personally?

Because it is a reflection of my self.

Is the art of design rooted in the art of life?

Design has to be user-friendly, not necessarily a piece of art. The objective of design is to see to it that people live in a better environment.

Which of these two guiding principles would you choose? Which one best reflects you and your attitude? "To give oneself" or "To know oneself"?

"To know oneself" – because I can know others only if I know myself. I cannot relate to other people's needs and wants if I don't know what I need and want for myself. Fashion, in the final analysis, is an aesthetic construct firmly based on functionality. Even "sexy" clothing serves a particular function.

How do you manage the transition from nothingness to an idea?

With words, collages, photos, bits and pieces, etc., to organize my research activities and to visualize my raw ideas.

Please finish the following sentence: To a designer, a new idea means …

… to raise a treasure. Actually, I'm afraid that I might run out of ideas someday. This is the reason why I, at this time, use each and every idea so as to design things the best I can. And it's just as important to learn how to keep oneself open for new things.

How do you remain open to inspiration?

I read books and magazines, I listen to a lot of music, I go out and constantly observe my environment.

What, in your opinion, is the greatest enemy of inspiration?

A noisy environment, a stressful atmosphere, and work without a recognizable sense or purpose. I never think about objects or persons that might have an adverse effect on my inspiration and creativity.

"A designer shouldn't live in his own small world, designed according to his own needs and wants; much rather, he should integrate his constantly changing environment into his work. Because that's the only place where the origin of creativity can be found."

When do you have your most creative moments?

I remember that, as a kid, I managed to invent ten different games which could all be played with one single piece of paper. That was the most creative moment I have ever experienced. But because we constantly learn new things and connect previous experiences with this newly-gained knowledge, I'm convinced that these creative moments will always recur.

How would you describe your working method? Is your work based exclusively on intuition? Does it all start with a feeling?

Feelings come and go. If I'm absolutely unable to feel something, I still try hard. I try to imagine it – hoping that I will hit upon some kind of connection between the objects and my mind. With "connection" I mean my previous observations, photos, pictures, etc.

Do you follow certain rituals in your work?

I always work with music in the background. That stimulates my brain.

Do you always work on only one idea at any given time?

No, because I have an easier time doing research with two or even three ideas in mind.

When are you most creative?

In the bathtub and right after I get up in the morning, at a time most people would rather stay in bed. At these two times of the day my head is absolutely free, and I'm capable of thinking clearly.

When does a designer know that he has a complete product: if nothing needs to be added to it?

That depends on the project. There is no general rule when to stop. Each design concept has its own rules.

What is a designer's most important tool?

Openness, so as to be able to welcome everything that's new.

How important is reduction in your concept of design?

This is, indeed, an important ability of all successful designers, because they know what is appropriate in any given situation, and what is not. "Less is more" – this is what we always have to keep in mind, and this is design at its best.

Could you describe your beginnings as a designer?

I felt like someone who wanted to communicate his thoughts and concepts but who was lacking the vocabulary to do so.

Do you have a favorite piece of clothing? And what secret lies behind it?

I like cardigans most. Each time I wear one I'm reminded of many things. In the beginning it was part of my school uniform, then there was one my sister knitted for me as a birthday present. I have worn it during many memorable moments, and whenever I wear a cardigan I feel the same kind of warmth and security.

Describe your favorite design object.

One of my mom's jackets which meant very much to her and which, to her, was associated with many memories.

Why should designers also be visionaries and create utopias?

Because we are empathetic and imaginative.

How do you go about realizing your design concepts?

It's different each time, and I don't follow a particular pattern of thought. Sometimes an idea emerges from a picture, and sometimes a person sparks it off. The visualization of thoughts, though, is the main step towards making design concepts become reality, because it is completely useless to keep one's ideas in one's head instead of using illustration media to work them out. Every designer should possess good visualization skills so that he can convey his idea to others. If this particular skill doesn't exist, there's no way to turn an idea into an actual design concept.

What do you think will be crucially important for the fashion industry in the years to come?

Market acceptance and open-minded customers.

Why will a designer never create something which is based exclusively on a beautiful form?

Because such people live in their own small world, unable to accept and tolerate anything else – not even themselves.

Does a design ever reach perfection?

Nothing is perfect! As designers, we have to give all of our expertise and our whole heart into the concept of the design. We must always try to make that particular concept the best there is. In the final analysis, it's the design which lets people recognize our passion, and we shouldn't be sorry for ourselves, because this recognition is already a kind of "perfect" reward for a designer.

Does creating fashion make sense at all if nobody can afford it?

Different cultures, different backgrounds, different life philosophies … it's all about personal viewpoints and approaches.

Why is elegance defined by simplicity?

Because every human being wants to be plain and simple in his inner self. It's really not that simple to maintain a plainness which is a blend of courage and the ability to show self-confidence to the outside world. This attitude and this self-confidence are perceived by others, and that is true elegance.

How do you define the "work of a designer"? Is it a give-and-take of ideas, knowledge, and arguments?

The "work of a designer" is not just about the "design" but also about "work." Each kind of work has its own set of rules, but they are quite fair and appropriate. I don't have any problems with that.

Are you free to experiment and learn at Norintra?

Yes, and being able to experiment helps me to keep learning.

When do you find the time to exchange ideas with other creative professionals?

I'd be able to find it if I were struggling with a certain design concept. But I don't like it when I'm still in the initial phase with raw ideas and think that everything must originate from oneself.

Do you, as a designer, find it difficult to work for a company and create objects which carry your personal touch and style?

It's a good opportunity to find out what my particular strengths are in different fashion domains. Everything depends on how much time and energy you invest in something and how you realize your vision accordingly.

Why is it a challenge for you to work for Norintra?

It's really a huge challenge for me. First, because my entire work experience is based on the local fashion retail business; here, the system and the working methods are completely different from former times. And secondly, because it's the first time I've been able to work with people on an international level.

Keeping your eyes open to the world around you is probably the best way to constantly obtain new inspiration.

ANGEL WONG PUI SHAN
A FASHION DESIGNER ALWAYS HAS
A VIEWPOINT OF HIS OWN

An interview with the designer

The fashion designer Angel Wong Pui Shan can strike the balance between her own style and customer requests, between working under time pressure, and creative development. In just a few months, she designed her own successful collection of eveningwear for Norintra that is both imaginative and wearable. She is always in search of new sources of inspiration. She says, "With the right inspirational basis, each of the models I work on becomes my favorite model. It is like an exciting treasure hunt full of expectation, resulting in lots of beautiful and unexpected things." The winner of the Hong Kong Young Fashion Designers' Contest trained as a design apprentice and then studied Fashion Design at the Hong Kong Polytechnic University. As a student, she designed ladies' fashion for the Together label of the Otto mail-order service.

The designer Angel Wong Pui Shan explains her idea for this model as follows: "This dress is inspired by the delicate petals of a flower. The designs reflect the different stages of the flower's blossoming."

What does creating fashion mean to you? Being torn between two completely different elements: calmness and stress, stimulation and inner composure …

Fashion design is actually a subject with many facets and aspects. In my view, it should neither be restricted nor be subjected to any kind of criteria.

Wolfgang Joop is firmly convinced that a fashion designer must have a feeling heart and eyes that have seen something of life. Do you share his view?

I do. Most designers, however, lack opportunities and implementation possibilities.

Is your fashion philosophy based on the cut?

I think the cut is but one of many elements. My work as a designer is influenced by the most diverse elements – such as different methods of manufacture, trimming, decoration, accessories.

Why should a fashion designer always be the harshest critic of his own ideas? To prevent him from becoming a slave of his first good idea?

A fashion designer always has a viewpoint of his own; he believes that his design concepts have their origins in his deepest inner self. He is absolutely convinced that he is not an opportunist – otherwise he wouldn't be a genuine creator.

What makes a creator of fashion an innovative designer?

Every designer has his own style so as to be groundbreaking and innovative. I believe that regular participation in fashion shows can be a great help. Because this particular environment can encourage a designer, and in addition there is the opportunity to exchange ideas with colleagues.

Do you consider yourself a kind of mediator between your own ideas and the customers' wishes and demands?

Yes, that is a basic prerequisite.

If it's the market that determines the image of a brand and the success of individual products, what role can you as a designer play in this process?

I can tackle the subject and find out how the image of a certain brand was established, and why. And I can also determine what elements a certain brand image is lacking.

Karl Lagerfeld once said that he wanted to deal with everyday problems as little as possible: "I'm an absolute egoist. My motto has always been: I'm the linchpin of everything that happens around me. To hell with everyone else." What do you think of this statement?

Just the fear of standing there alone at some point would keep me from being so egoistic. Of course, I admire people who are self-confident, but the self-confidence should be natural and "inborn". It's like a design concept where talent is crucial. "I'm the linchpin of everything that happens around me" – this shows a high level of responsibility. If I draw up a design that will be completed by someone else, the approach – compared to the original idea – is totally different. As long as the decision maker does not explicitly wish an "aha!" effect, the result won't necessarily meet the designer's original expectations.

Isn't designing like a trip into the unknown, with the designer uncertain whether he'll ever arrive at his destination because the travel route is constantly changing?

If the essential purpose of the designer's work is to create a planned or desired effect, then this is a goal which I would like to achieve. If, on the other hand, the designer's work is characterized by flexibility, with sufficient space for creativity, I wouldn't be bothered by unexpected twists and turns, because I could expect a surprising result at the end of the journey.

What is more important to you: the process (the journey) or the product (the arrival)?

If enough time is arranged for the design process, it's always a real pleasure for me. I can concentrate better so as to arrive at a satisfactory result. If, on the other hand, the timeline is tight it can certainly happen that I don't try new approaches in order to finish in time. If I had the choice, I would undoubtedly favor the process.

Why is designing so important to you personally?

In my view, designers have a right to creativity, but at the same time they have to assume responsibility for the result. This is why a designer's work can quickly turn into a personal concern.

Is the art of design rooted in the art of life?

My work as a designer is inspired by things, persons, and events in my environment. It is really a great help to search for new things during the design process, and to explore these novelties.

Which of these two guiding principles would you choose? Which one best reflects you and your attitude? "To give oneself" or "To know oneself"?

At the outset of my design career I was very interested in "knowing myself." Now, however, with a certain person in mind (for example, the customer), I want to involve my personality in the work and to "give myself."

How do you manage the transition from nothingness to an idea?

To me personally, the word "nothing" does not exist in a designer's vocabulary. It should be replaced by the word "infinity."

Please finish the following sentence: To a designer, a new idea means …

… a decision.

How do you remain open to inspiration?

By keeping up the pleasure and the curiosity connected with events happening all over the world. This includes, for example, that I actively approach friends for an exchange of ideas, keeping myself open to different viewpoints. This is the basic prerequisite for being able to "find" new avenues.

What, in your opinion, is the greatest enemy of inspiration?

Time.

When do you have your most creative moments?

I always think that my most creative moments are still to come. That's why I always hope that each new design concept will be better than the previous one. This causes me to constantly move ahead.

How would you describe your working method? Is your work based exclusively on intuition? Does it all start with a feeling?

Intuition and feeling are, when it comes to my own work, the second step. They are always preceded by listening, assimilating, and asking.

Do you follow certain rituals in your work?

Not really, because I set a high value on variety in my ideas, and I like to try new things. I think that continuity is based on continuous change.

Do you always work on only one idea at any given time?

That's impossible for me.

How does a designer know that he has a complete product? When there is nothing that can be added to it?

I love this question. Each design concept renders the impression that there is nothing which can be added to it, or improved. A designer in the learning or experiential phase should be allowed his own reasons, and even the right, to make his own decisions. In general, other people's objections or comments should therefore be taken into consideration.

What is a designer's most important tool?

To me, the most important tool is to find the right way, that is, to formulate the actual message of the design concept in such a way that others will be able to comprehend it as well. The full significance of his design concept, though, will only be revealed to the designer himself.

How important is reduction in your concept of design?

I think this refers to the process of recognizing exactly what I want and what will suit that purpose.

Could you describe your beginnings as a designer?

In my early years I always asked myself who I am. I wanted to "get to know myself" by all means, and to explore my strengths and weaknesses.

"My work as a designer is inspired by things, people, and by events in my environment. It is really very helpful to look for and explore new things during the design process."

What, in your view, makes a piece of clothing timeless and independent of trends?

This particular subject is causing quite a stir with many people, and some designer labels are insisting on their own special course and style. If a designer wants to create fashion clothing which is special and independent of trends, he should always stay true to his own personal style, but he should also take the sales arguments of the design into consideration. With regard to this aspect, Vivien Tam is particularly successful. She has managed to integrate Chinese culture into her design concepts so adroitly that her works are anchored firmly in the people's memory.

Do your creations follow trends, or are you the one who sets the trends?

My creations at Norintra are not intended for my own personal label, so I orient myself, first of all, to the criteria set by the customer. I adjust my work accordingly so as to fulfill the respective requirements.

Do you have a favorite piece of clothing? And what secret lies behind it?

Jeans are one of my favorite pieces of clothing. They can easily be combined with other pieces of clothing, and they're timeless. They can be worn day and night – no matter if it's a casual sports event or a special occasion.

Describe your favorite design object.

With the right inspiration as basis, every design concept I am working on turns into my favorite concept. It's like an exciting treasure hunt full of expectations, bringing about many beautiful and unexpected things.

Why should designers also be visionaries and create utopias?

Designers have the talent to generate specific ideas with their creative potential by seeing, thinking, and feeling, and to communicate these ideas to other people. One can also say that designers live in utopias – or better: live a utopia.

How do you go about realizing your design concepts?

I think I have a fine sense of perception when it comes to the

question of why people want fashion: either they have a basic desire for it, or they simply want to wear a certain model and design.

Do you agree with the statement that a creative design concept incorporates what you see in yourself and in front of yourself?

Yes, I agree. This is so because the source point of all creativity is always a thought of one's own. Even if the design has to satisfy commercial demands, the designer's work always starts with his personal concept, and only then will it be implemented, together with the commercial elements required, to a final design concept.

What do you think will be crucially important for the fashion industry in the years to come?

Environmental protection will continue to be an important subject in the years to come. It would be good to accent the personal touch of a collection instead of strictly following the trends only. It would also be a good sales argument to introduce new ideas for the use of environmentally friendly materials.

Why will a designer never create something which is based exclusively on a beautiful form?

When it comes to beauty, every person has his own yardstick. One person prefers simple, plain clothing, another person favors garish design which, in the eyes of a third person, would perhaps be considered hideous.

What does style mean to you? Is it the expression of your own personality?

That doesn't fully explain it, even though a small part of my personality may become visible at times.

How would you describe the style of your current eveningwear collection?

The eveningwear designed by me is intended for different types of women who have their own unmistakable style and character. My approach is that I don't just design beautiful evening dresses, because that's not enough. The most important element here is to decide on a suitable and appropriate cut. If, for example, a woman is aware of her impeccable and beautiful back, then a backless evening dress with a sexy cutout is the right choice.

How did you come up with the ideas for your eveningwear collection? What inspired and motivated you?

When I start designing a new collection I first collect all the relevant information from different sources, such as the Internet, from magazines, people in the street, or whatever I'm trying out at the time. I'm glad I live in an international city like Hong Kong. This makes it easy to obtain the very latest information from around the world whenever I need it. And this cultural background is also very helpful to me when it comes to understanding the needs and wants of people in different countries

How important is the romantic world of poetry to you? Which motifs from the world of art and literature can be found in your eveningwear collection? In your design concepts one often sees a swan; in fact, your clothes are an allusion to a swan spreading its wings, and this is the start of a fairy-tale episode in life … Is this what you intended with this approach?

Yes, that's on my mind, too. I think that when women go to a party they also have romantic feelings – and they expect to enjoy the next few hours.

What is so fascinating about the swan motif for fashion designers? Is it the notion of metamorphosis? Wolfgang Joop, by the way, once compared himself to the youngest of the princes in the Hans Christian Andersen fairy tale "The Wild Swans" who, not totally released from the spell cast on him, has a swan's wing instead of a human arm, because his mail shirt was lacking a sleeve. The whole tale is characterized by the notion of imperfection and painful metamorphosis. Can the designer be creative only when he is searching for something that he himself is lacking?

In my opinion, it is difficult to coherently define the meaning of "creative." But I would like to use this point to express one of my beliefs: it is important that a designer be able to successfully try new things and create new design concepts.

You are associating your evening collection with a "precious moment." What are the precious moments in life for you?

One precious moment in my life was when I was awarded the prize of overall winner at the 2005 Hong Kong Young Fashion Designers' Contest. This opened my eyes to all the different kinds of people and things. I also realized that a creative job is not a lonesome job.

How do you deal with the attribute "sexy" when it comes to your collection?

People express feelings which sometimes also convey a kind of sexy temper or spirit. If I work on a design concept I keep an eye on the character and feelings of people. I always think of the things that people wearing my design concepts might wish, and sometimes I try to imagine that I am that person. A design concept is not merely a "thing" – it is full of life, and of course it is possible for the erotic charisma of a piece of clothing to transfer to the person wearing it.

What do you think is the most sensuous material? Silk, the "Queen of Fabrics"?

For eveningwear, I choose silk because this material easily reflects what we associate with "sexy." For business attire, I choose linen and cotton because these materials help to accentuate the charm of cosmopolitical businesswomen. In any case, my answer for different designs is the correct selection of various materials.

Do you have a favorite color?

My favorite color is white – a friendly color which can easily be used with all other colors.

When do you feel understood as a designer?

Ever since I came to understand the actual tasks of our business I have also understood what it means to be a designer. I will always make sure that I understand what the customer really wants, and it's important to know how to filter out personal ideas, concepts, and comments. Most designers, by the way, do not refer to themselves merely as designers but also as artists.

There's a book by Johannes Mario Simmel called "The Stuff That Dreams Are Made Of." What stuff are your dreams made of?

My dreams can be summarized in five words: joy, indulgence, interest, sharing, and surprise.

Does a design ever reach perfection?

I don't really focus on whether a design concept is perfect but merely on whether my design sparks a certain fascination.

At the Kulturförderpreis culture awards ceremony in Berlin: the German TV presenter Marietta Slomka congratulates the designer Angel Wong Pui Shan on her collection of evening wear.

Does creating fashion make sense at all if nobody can afford it?

I think there are two criteria that have to be considered here. If fashion is considered unaffordable because of its price, I can't really comment on this because people also have different viewpoints in this regard. But if fashion clothing can't be worn because of the person's figure, style or character, I'd be glad to help out.

Why is elegance defined by simplicity?

To me, elegance can't be equated with many accessories, decorations, and adornments. Elegance can only be a person's temperament or disposition.

How do you define the "work of a designer"? Is it a give-and-take of ideas, knowledge, and arguments?

I think there are several professional fields which have their own give-and-take processes. For a designer, a positive professional attitude is always the key to success.

Are you free to experiment and learn at Norintra?

It depends: if customers have specific objectives which I'm supposed to implement on a precise one-to-one basis, then it's more a case of passive work that does not leave much space for my own creativity. If, on the other hand, I'm invited to come up with ideas for the implementation of the customers' initial ideas, I become more active as there's more space to be creative.

Do you, as a designer, find it difficult to work for a company and create objects which carry your personal touch and style?

I don't have any problem with that at all. If I decide to work for a company, then I'm totally aware of the fact that I have to orient myself to that company. My role in this position is to create design concepts which meet the demands of that company. It's definitely possible to combine "personal touch" with "corporate design" and to bring about a "corporate touch." Designers who want to create their own fashion exclusively should do that under their own label.

Why is it a challenge for you to work for Norintra?

I guess the lifeblood of every young designer revolves around the path leading "from zero to complete realization of the design concept," At Norintra, a still very young company founded in March 2007, I can walk that path. I see a vast number of opportunities and chances to find fulfillment.

BARBARA SKUCZIK
ACTUALLY, I'M ALWAYS CREATIVE

An interview with the designer

"Designing a simple and beautiful piece of clothing is one of the greatest challenges there is, and goes hand in hand with absolute mastery of one's trade." – Barbara Skuczik is a master of her trade. She has already worked as a fashion and textile designer for such established fashion labels as Louis Vuitton, Marc by Marc Jacobs, See by Chloe, Chanel, Diane von Fürstenberg, Oscar by Oscar de la Renta or Victoria's Secret. According to the young designer, it is important in her line of work to constantly keep her eyes open, always gaining new experiences that can then be worked into her models. "You can see a lot without travelling far" – that's the motto of this young designer, yet she herself was born in Poland in 1976, grew up in Germany, studied in London at the London College of Fashion and Central St. Martins, and lived and worked in London and Paris before coming to Hong Kong to work in an international team for Norintra House of Fashion.

What does creating fashion mean to you? Being torn between two completely different elements: calmness and stress, stimulation and inner composure …

Designing fashion is my job, and I am really having a lot of fun with it. I'm very happy to enjoy the privilege of working in this profession.

Wolfgang Joop is firmly convinced that a fashion designer must have a feeling heart and eyes that have seen something of life. Do you share his view?

Yes, a designer must have a sophisticated sense of perception, and he has to be able to consciously perceive what is happening around him. A person can have seen many things without taking distant journeys, and we all should have a compassionate heart.

Is your fashion philosophy based on the cut?

The cut is of crucial significance to fashion design. It creates the form and bestows life to the piece of clothing. The wrong fabric or a flawed realization, however, can spoil the most beautiful cut. It's of utmost importance to take all factors into consideration.

Why should a fashion designer always be the harshest critic of his own ideas? To prevent him from becoming a slave of his first good idea?

A good idea always sets off a domino effect which proceeds in different directions. Fashion designers are trained in this particular thought process; they're choosy and focus on the essentials.

What makes a creator of fashion an innovative designer?

A vision and the ability to put it into effect.

Do you consider yourself a kind of mediator between your own ideas and the customers' wishes and demands?

The hallmark of a good designer is his experience and ability to give consideration to customers' wishes, yet at the same time to give the product his personal touch.

If it's the market that determines the image of a brand and the success of individual products, what role can you as a designer play in this process?

That depends on the brand itself and on the degree of freedom that I'm allowed as a designer.

Karl Lagerfeld once said that he wanted to deal with everyday problems as little as possible: "I'm an absolute egoist. My motto has always been: I'm the linchpin of everything that happens around me. To hell with everyone else." What do you think of this statement?

Obviously, this motto served him well, so I can't say very much about it. I personally think we all would like to do without everyday problems, but that's a luxury only a very few of us can afford.

Isn't designing like a trip into the unknown, with the designer uncertain whether he'll ever arrive at his destination because the travel route is constantly changing?

Yes, this is often the case.

What is more important to you: the process (the journey) or the product (the arrival)?

I personally take much joy in the "journey," because this is the part which allows me to be creative as a fashion designer. Seeing the final product, in particular when a customer is wearing it out in the street, is just a great feeling.

Why is designing so important to you personally?

Because it's my big passion.

Is the art of design rooted in the art of life?

Certainly. We must not forget, however, that everybody lives according to his or her own style.

Which of these two guiding principles would you choose? Which one best reflects you and your attitude? "To give oneself" or "To know oneself"?

I believe that, first of all, one has to give oneself and exploit one's creativity to the utmost limits before one can then get to know oneself as a designer.

Hong Kong offers the best prerequisites for those in the creative field: it is a lively city, a melting pot of hugely different influences – a metropolis for new ideas.

When designing this dress, the designer Angel Wong Pui Shan took her
inspiration from the sea, from gentle waves breaking and sparkling.

"The cut is of crucial significance to fashion design. It creates the
form and bestows life to the piece of clothing."

How do you manage the transition from nothingness to an idea?

In my case, ideas can be evoked by the most different things.

Please finish the following sentence: To a designer, a new idea means …

… more work.

How do you remain open to inspiration?

With constant curiosity.

What, in your opinion, is the greatest enemy of inspiration?

If one starts to become lazy, slack off, and revert to old habits.

When do you have your most creative moments?

When I'm out and about.

How would you describe your working method? Is your work based exclusively on intuition? Does it all start with a feeling?

Yes, intuition and a feeling for what is happening around me both play an important role.

Do you follow certain rituals in your work?

Fashion designers have to follow certain steps in their work. It's more a process than a ritual.

Do you always work on only one idea at any given time?

No, because there just isn't enough time for that. But I like to work on different projects at the same time.

When are you most creative?

Actually, I'm always creative. That doesn't refer to my work only. For example, I like to be creative in the kitchen; it's the perfect place for me to relax. As I'm not a master chef, though, it's rather unlikely that I will ever gain a foothold in that particular field.

How does a designer know that he has a complete product? When there is nothing that can be added to it?

Sometimes one has to cancel things in order to arrive at a satisfactory result. In general, however, there are no specific rules. I personally think that one knows when a product is complete by looking at it.

What is a designer's most important tool?

Self-confidence during the realization of his ideas.

How important is reduction in your concept of design?

Above all else, I try not to add anything superfluous.

Could you describe your beginnings as a designer?

It might sound strange, but I really liked the period of uncertainty right after my graduation from university. At that time, everything revolved around my creativity, and I greatly enjoyed working together with other young designers.

What is it that, in your view, makes a piece of clothing timeless and independent of trends?

It must be an object of desire.

Do you have a favorite piece of clothing? And what secret lies behind it?

My favorite pieces of clothing have a certain sentimental value attached to them.

Describe your favorite design object.

It's an old, silk chiffon dress I bought at Portobello Market when I came to London for the first time as a student of fashion design.

Why should designers also be visionaries and create utopias?

It is so exciting to see these fantasy creations on the catwalks – creations which are not necessarily intended for sale in stores. Such creations are much rather reflections of certain moods or feelings the designer wishes to express. The final product can be very appealing.

How do you go about realizing your design concepts?

It's important to stay focused and to use all resources available in an optimum way so as to realize the desired product.

What do you think will be crucially important for the fashion industry in the years to come?

In my opinion, it's really important that fashion companies maintain their individuality. Today, trends change with ever increasing speed, and by no means should they determine or even dominate the collections – at best they should act as an inspiration.

Does a design ever reach perfection?

The act of designing is a never-ending process.

Does creating fashion make sense at all if nobody can afford it?

Well, if there is still a market for it, why not?

Why is elegance defined by simplicity?

It's one of the biggest challenges to design a plain and beautiful piece of clothing; this goes hand in glove with the absolute mastery of design craftsmanship. Elegance is not restricted to times or places. And the same holds good for design concepts.

How do you define the "work of a designer"? Is it a give-and-take of ideas, knowledge, and arguments?

In my opinion, this is the case in all respects.

When do you find the time to exchange ideas with other creative professionals?

This happens whenever I encounter expertise, for example, at fashion fairs.

Do you, as a designer, consider it difficult to work for a company and create objects which carry your personal touch and style?

No – I like to design fashion for a certain market. That's a new and different experience which I find exciting and challenging.

Why is it a challenge for you to work for Norintra?

I've already lived and worked in London and Paris, but I believe that I'm now living in the right place at the right time. And in addition, I have the chance to design products for Germany.

Teamwork is a must in order to deliver creative results.

"Yes, a designer must have a sophisticated sense of perception, and he has to be able to consciously perceive what is happening around him. A person can have seen many things without taking distant journeys, and we all should have a compassionate heart."

PAMELA WU CHUI PIK
MY FASHION PHILOSOPHY IS BASED ON MY LIFESTYLE

An interview with the designer

Many fashion creators and designers say that they were interested in fashion even as children and designed their first models while they were youngsters, in other words, that they never wanted to be anything other than a fashion designer. Not so for Pamela Wu Chui Pik: "I actually come from the field of graphics and fashion photography, which was a lot of fun but also extremely hard work. And then I fell in love with designing fashion." The designer initially studied Fashion Design in Hong Kong, where she worked as a designer for a few years before moving to London to complete her bachelors and masters degrees at Middlesex und Westminster universities. During this time she designed clothes for Vivian Westwood, Shelley Fox, Victims, Debi Hall, Selfridges, and Justina of London, among others, before returning to Hong Kong in 2006. She is fascinated by the constant transitions in fashion, by novelty, and by the entire process. This is also why she feels that a company with too many limitations on design and the designers cannot be hugely successful.

What does creating fashion mean to you? Being torn between two completely different elements: calmness and stress, stimulation and inner composure …

Fashion articles are aesthetic objects that are deeply rooted in art and history. Over the course of years, fashion has left its specific footprints in human culture. It's almost impossible to determine the era when clothes were no longer just a necessity of everyday life but became an object of desire.

Wolfgang Joop is firmly convinced that a fashion designer must have a feeling heart and eyes that have seen something of life. Do you share his view?

If you set your heart on something and are affectively engaged in it you won't lose your way.

Is your fashion philosophy based on the cut?

My fashion philosophy is based on my lifestyle.

Why should a fashion designer always be the harshest critic of his own ideas? To prevent him from becoming a slave of his first good idea?

Always calling yourself into question is the best way to bring the quality of design to perfection.

What makes a fashion designer an innovative designer?

There are several conditions to establish the characteristic "signature" of a designer. First of all, he has to create his own image, assert his individuality, and then effectively communicate it. Afterwards, he has to outline a specific customer group, understand the market, and identify the customers.

Do you consider yourself a kind of mediator between your own ideas and the customers' wishes and demands?

No, not at all.

If it's the market that determines the image of a brand and the success of individual products, what role can you as a designer play in this process?

For many companies, the product mix and assortment are key elements of their business strategy. To expand the product mix you need more product versions. That's why designers have to offer a successful diversification of the brand image and the products in order to obtain a better market penetration.

"I like the entire design process more than the product itself, because the end product reflects only part of the whole process."

Karl Lagerfeld once said that he wanted to deal with everyday problems as little as possible: "I'm an absolute egoist. My motto has always been: I'm the linchpin of everything that happens around me. To hell with everyone else." What do you think of this statement?

Fashion doesn't start with me, and it will surely not end with me.

Isn't designing like a trip into the unknown, with the designer uncertain whether he'll ever arrive at his destination because the travel route is constantly changing?

The term "fashion" is self-defining and its very meaning corresponds to "constant change" – like Earth rotating constantly. I simply can't imagine that it will ever come to a halt. That's exactly why I'm so fascinated by fashion.

What is more important to you: the process (the journey) or the product (the arrival)?

I take more pleasure in the entire design process than I do in the product itself. The final product actually expresses only part of the whole and I'm personally learning more from the process.

Why is designing so important to you personally?

Designing is one of the non-verbal possibilities of self-interpretation.

Is the art of design rooted in the art of life?

Yes, absolutely. Let me quote Barnard Malcolm in this context: "Since the beginning of the 20th century, modernity has conquered the world, and a global culture of modernity is to be found in thoughts and art."

Which of these two guiding principles would you choose? Which one best reflects you and your attitude? "To give oneself" or "To know oneself"?

To understand myself.

How do you manage the transition from nothingness to an idea?

To a larger extent, inspiration originates in visual arts and in experimenting with materials and colors. These two main elements are incorporated in clothing and play an important role in reflecting and mirroring contemporary life.

Please finish the following sentence: To a designer, a new idea means …

… something valuable.

How do you remain open to inspiration?

My deep passion is my guarantee for it.

What, in your opinion, is the greatest enemy of inspiration?

Setting myself boundaries.

When do you have your most creative moments?

At night, in silence, alone, when daydreaming, by visionary chance …

How would you describe your working method? Is your work based exclusively on intuition? Does it all start with a feeling?

I'm pretty well organized. That's why intuition or mere feelings play a rather secondary role when starting with my work.

Do you follow certain rituals in your work?

I do research, pick something out as a central theme, and then I devote myself to colors.

Do you always work on only one idea at any given time?

I always work on several tasks, but as far as possible only on one idea at a time.

When are you most creative?

Outside the studio.

How does a designer know that he has a complete product? When there is nothing that can be added to it?

When the focus, the key detail, has been successfully integrated and expressed in design.

What is a designer's most important tool?

Self-motivation and the passion for design.

How important is reduction in your concept of design?

"Less is more" – this is always true.

Could you describe your beginnings as a designer?

Actually, I originally worked in graphics and fashion photography – that was great fun, but at the same time extremely hard work ... I learned a lot there, especially to control my temper. Well, I then fell in love with creating fashion.

Do you have a favorite piece of clothing? And what secret lies behind it?

Jeans – they combine beautifully with my clothing. Today, jeans have the image of a recognized couture element.

Describe your favorite design object.

Anything that originates from the "minimalism" movement and is constructive – especially the sculpture installations by Andy Goldsworthy.

Why should designers also be visionaries and create utopias?

When I look at something from a distance my vision broadens and I get to know more.

How do you go about realizing your design concepts?

By integrating experience made in the past.

What do you think will be crucially important for the fashion industry in the years to come?

Globalization.

Why will a designer never create something which is based exclusively on a beautiful form?

Democracy in arts and design creates an open definition of the beauty of a form.

Does a design ever reach perfection?

I'm used to making the best of everything and nothing.

"The term 'fashion' is self-defining and its very meaning corresponds to 'constant change' – like Earth rotating constantly. I simply can't imagine that it will ever come to a halt. That's exactly why I'm so fascinated by fashion."

If is very difficult to create a perfect model, because there is always a struggle between creativity and reality.

Inspiration can come from all sorts of sources: India's rich culture with its palaces and noble estates was the inspiration for this embroidered evening dress by Angel Wong Pui Shan.

Does creating fashion make sense at all if nobody can afford it?

With regard to fashion design there should be no limits – only those set by Hans Christian Andersen's fairy tale "The Emperor's New Clothes."

Why is elegance defined by simplicity?

In my opinion, simplicity is defined by classical values, timelessness, and quality.

How do you define the "work of a designer"? Is it a give-and-take of ideas, knowledge, and arguments?

It's an exchange of ideas between sellers and buyers; it's self-awareness and the difficult communication between creativity and reality.

Are you free to experiment and learn at Norintra?

I'm learning to exploit my creativity under certain restricting conditions such as price specifications or minimum quantities.

When do you find the time to exchange ideas with other creative professionals?

I learn from history, I read, I like to surf on the Internet, to travel, visit galleries and exhibitions, go shopping, etc. A great deal too many opportunities.

Do you, as a designer, find it difficult to work for a company and create objects which carry your personal touch and style?

A company with too many restrictions for designs or designers will not be overly successful. Depending on the creative level, a "personal touch" is always added.

Why is it a challenge for you to work for Norintra?

Because it's a matter of designing different kinds of ladies' wear. Further challenges are to match tight time schedules and meet high quality requirements, cooperation in the team, as well as quality controls and checks.

JEFF WU KOON HOO
A FASHION DESIGNER FEELS PAIN WITHOUT BEING WOUNDED

An interview with the designer

Jeff Wu Koon Hoo is always on the move, constantly searching for fresh ideas and working against the clock because "If you don't want to miss the 'trend boat,' you can't afford to stop for a pause." He is an "imperfect perfectionist" because he believes that a designer can never be satisfied with his or her own models and is always in search of unattainable perfection. For Jeff Wu Koon Hoo, for example, this perfection involves achieving maximum effects with minimalist details in men's fashion. When asked about his early days as a designer, Jeff Wu Koon Hoo admits readily that he was a "copier." The 27-year-old studied Industrial and Commercial Design at the Design First Institute and at the Haking Wong Technical Institute, and went on to study Digital Media at the Kung Tong Technical Institute. He has been working as a fashion designer in the clothing industry since 2002, and has created designs for Charlies Int. and Lachmis Int. Nowadays, he sees his greatest challenge as "clothing" his ideas in the wishes of his customers.

"Fashion is not simply a visual concept but rather a constant reflection of society. It is complicated and multi-facetted – a projection of the social climate at a given time. Any designer who wants to get the hang of fashion must understand the demographic currents of a society."

What does creating fashion mean to you? Being torn between two completely different elements: calmness and stress, stimulation and inner composure …

Fashion is not simply a visual concept but rather a constant reflection of society. It is complicated and multi-facetted – a projection of the social climate at a given time. Any designer who wants to get the hang of fashion must understand the demographic currents of a society.

Wolfgang Joop is firmly convinced that a fashion designer must have a feeling heart and eyes that have seen something of life. Do you share his view?

A fashion designer feels pain without being wounded, sees stars when the sky is clouded – normally he perceives beauty in the most profane objects and successfully realizes his vision in a piece of clothing.

Is your fashion philosophy based on the cut?

When you're a fashion designer for male clothing the challenge is to create minimal "maximum designs." This statement may seem to be a contradiction in itself but it represents the essential basic understanding, which in my opinion all designers of male fashion have to internalize: minimal details resulting in maximum visual effect.

Why should a fashion designer always be the harshest critic of his own ideas? To prevent him from becoming a slave of his first good idea?

Its sounds odd, but sometimes the first ideas are the best. A designer doesn't need to be self-critical all the time. He has to learn to find out when and where to stop being self-critical and be content. I can say with certainty that no designer will ever be content with his drafts. We're all looking for an impossible perfection. Trying to be a perfect fashion maker is not at all perfect, because fashion is a fast-changing branch. It's important to understand this. If you want to be in the right place at the right time as far as trends are concerned, then you can't afford to stop for a pause.

What makes a creator of fashion an innovative designer?

By thinking beyond any templates.

Do you consider yourself a kind of mediator between your own ideas and the customers' wishes and demands?

Yes, indeed. The clients are my partners at the "scene of the crime." They set the scene and I orchestrate the event accordingly.

If it's the market that determines the image of a brand and the success of individual products, what role can you as a designer play in this process?

As a designer I have to be able to perfectly comprehend the brand image, the market, and the clients' wishes. I always work closely with those in market research and I gather bestseller information to obtain and maximize our share of the market.

Karl Lagerfeld once said that he wanted to deal with everyday problems as little as possible: "I'm an absolute egoist. My motto has always been: I'm the linchpin of everything that happens around me. To hell with everyone else." What do you think of this statement?

I don't agree with this statement because it would contradict my previous statements. Designers depend on consumers in order to survive. Even Karl Lagerfeld has to admit that his clients do not buy "his" concepts but rather the image of the brand he is managing. He enjoys the luxury of being able to work under the protection and security of Chanel.

Isn't designing like a trip into the unknown, with the designer uncertain whether he'll ever arrive at his destination because the travel route is constantly changing?

To create design resembles a journey of self-discovery.

What is more important to you: the process (the journey) or the product (the arrival)?

The process is interesting and connected to the exploration of many unknown things. The product arrival is exciting and sometimes connected with unexpected working results.

Why is designing so important to you personally?

Designing need not be a personal issue as long as it's not a matter of my own personal label. That should not be the case at all! I'd never find a job if I made designing a personal matter.

Most certainly. Ideas that influence my creative output have their roots in experiences from my everyday life.

Which of these two guiding principles would you choose? Which one best reflects you and your attitude? "To give oneself" or "To know oneself"?

Discover yourself.

How do you manage the transition from nothingness to an idea?

There is never a nothing setting off an idea because nothingness in itself is already a certain conception you can start with.

Please finish the following sentence: To a designer, a new idea means …

… money.

How do you remain open to inspiration?

By keeping an open mind.

What, in your opinion, is the greatest enemy of inspiration?

Prejudice and mere commerce.

When do you have your most creative moments?

I think it's in the morning – there is more inspiration and there are new ideas because it's the beginning of a very new day.

How would you describe your working method? Is your work based exclusively on intuition? Does it all start with a feeling?

A solid concept or subject is an important starting point. Without schedule, it is difficult for a designer to navigate in these unsafe waters.

Do you follow certain rituals in your work?

Not really. I'm happy to have a profession that is also my hobby! It's important to take pleasure in your profession because we spent a lot of time with it.

Do you always work on only one idea at any given time?

I wish this were true!

When are you most creative?

In the morning, if I have slept well. The beginning is always refreshing and exciting, as it may be the case with a relationship … before it begins to get too complicated …

How does a designer know that he has a complete product? When there is nothing that can be added to it?

A designer is never content with his draft. This is the frustrating part.

What is a designer's most important tool?

The designer's personality determines which paths he will follow. There is a constant flow of information in his environment. The selection of information a designer memorizes for later use decides on how this information will influence his creative thinking. Designers should always watch their environment with a tolerant and open mind.

Could you describe your beginnings as a designer?

I was a copyist!

What do you think makes a piece of clothing timeless and independent of trends.

"Simplicity is the soul of elegance."

Do you have a favorite piece of clothing? And what secret lies behind it?

Denim jeans! Because I got them when I visited Japan for the first time.

Describe your favorite design object.

A design that speaks for itself.

"The customers are my partners at the 'scene of the crime.' They provide the setting, and I orchestrate the events accordingly."

"In order to implement a model design, it is important to have a good understanding of colors, shapes, fabrics, and technical design."

How do you go about realizing your design concepts?

To realize a conceptual draft a solid understanding of colors, fabrics, and technical construction is important. Nothing would ever succeed if I were incapable of communicating to a technician how to transform my two-dimensional ideas into a three-dimensional shape. That would like the blind leading the blind.

What do you think will be crucially important for the fashion industry in the years to come?

The ideal case would be fantastic: if the industry could disengage itself from safety thinking and mere commerce in general. I think there are too many rules and restrictions in a branch that ironically should be free of such restrictions.

Why will a designer never create something which is based exclusively on a beautiful form?

Because all people love beautiful things.

Does a design ever reach perfection?

Certainly, if a product were not perfect I would not present it on the market.

Does creating fashion make sense at all if nobody can afford it?

Well, certainly! Designers lend expression to dreams and wishes. And designers' ideas, which nobody can afford, are diluted into mainstream products by chain stores, anyway. As designers, we make the world we live in much more interesting.

Why is elegance defined by simplicity?

Because elegance comes from inside. Clothing only emphasizes what the wearer already possesses.

How do you define the "work of a designer"? Is it a give-and-take of ideas, knowledge, and arguments?

It's expert knowledge.

Are you free to experiment and learn at Norintra?

Yes, I am.

When do you find the time to exchange ideas with other creative professionals?

When it's time to do so, and when I would like more stimulii.

Do you, as a designer, find it difficult to work for a company and create objects which carry your personal touch and style?

No.

Why is it a challenge for you to work for Norintra?

Because I have to "clothe" my ideas with the conceptions of my clients.

KEVIN NG WAI LOK
DESIGNING IS A PROCESS

An interview with the designer

Kevin Ng Wai Lok sees fashion as a means of expressing himself. In his own words, the designer explains this as follows: "Fashion is one of the most fundamental means of expression that we can use to show the extent to which we have decided to conform to cultural norms or diverge from these – in other words, how prepared we are to 'integrate' or 'stand out from the crowd.'" Kevin Ng Wai Lok was born in Hong Kong in 1972. After completing his Bachelor of Arts at the Polytechnic University, he started his career with a presentation at a talent competition, and won the Wool Prize at the Hong Kong Young Designers' Show in 1998. This early success was followed in 1999/2000 by a special distinction at the Osaka Fashion Competition. In recognition of his broad-based talent, Kevin was given the opportunity to work as a designer for various well-known brands, including Esprit (edc) and IT (izzue). He has devoted his creativity and wealth of ideas to Norintra, but also has his own two labels, the "Shhh" brand, based on unique creations, and the streetwear line "Wasabi."

"The model is nothing more and nothing less than a process!"

What does creating fashion mean to you? Being torn between two completely different elements: calmness and stress, stimulation and inner composure ...

The creation of fashion includes an active fusion of two extreme elements which the self, on the one hand, identifies as unique and which, on the other hand, it associates with acceptance. The degree to which designers use these elements – individuality and fusion – for themselves is a challenge because the correct balance must be found so as to arrive at the desired design objective.

Wolfgang Joop is firmly convinced that a fashion designer must have a feeling heart and eyes that have seen something of life. Do you share his view?

Yes, it depends on a heart which feels differently, and on eyes looking beyond profane things, and the ability to express what one feels and sees.

Is your fashion philosophy based on the cut?

My fashion philosophy is based on manipulation.

Why should a fashion designer always be the harshest critic of his own ideas? To prevent him from becoming a slave of his first good idea?

Designing is a process – no more and no less!

What makes a creator of fashion an innovative designer?

A passionate heart, an open way of looking at things, and endurance.

Do you consider yourself a kind of mediator between your own ideas and the customers' wishes and demands?

This applies in about forty percent of all cases.

If it's the market that determines the image of a brand and the success of individual products, what role can you as a designer play in this process?

The creation of a brand image and the success of individual products are always an interplay between market and designer. None of them functions by itself.

"To know oneself is a really interesting and challenging process – an ultimate goal in life."

What is more important to you: the process (the journey) or the product (the arrival)?

Our whole life is a process – including designing. You guide the process, and it will guide you in turn. A good process course means good products!

Is the art of design rooted in the art of life?

The art of "everything" is always the same: it always gives us more than anything material can give us.

Which of these two guiding principles would you choose? Which one best reflects you and your attitude? "To give oneself" or "To know oneself"?

To know oneself is a really interesting and challenging process – an ultimate goal in life. If one doesn't know oneself, how can one then "give oneself" – what is there to give?

How do you manage the transition from nothingness to an idea?

By deciphering and subsequent processing.

Please finish the following sentence: To a designer, a new idea means …

… a beginning.

How do you remain open to inspiration?

By staying young mentally – that is, being open-minded to new things.

What, in your opinion, is the greatest enemy of inspiration?

If one allows oneself to grow old – that is, to stagnate and to cling on to old habits.

How would you describe your working method? Is your work based exclusively on intuition? Does it all start with a feeling?

Designing is a problem-solving process! First you get yourself in trouble, and then things start working out.

Do you always work on only one idea at any given time?

No, that's impossible for me.

"A beautiful form all by itself can be a pleasure only to the eye – a concept and a significance, on the other hand, please the soul."

The fashion designer makes the transition from nothingness to the idea by "deciphering and then processing these thoughts."

For Kevin Ng Wai Lok, fashion is one of the most fundamental means of expression.

How does a designer know that he has a complete product? When there is nothing that can be added to it?

When the problem is solved.

What is a designer's most important tool?

Feeling.

How important is reduction in your concept of design?

Just as important as other things.

Could you describe your beginnings as a designer?

I felt like a baby.

Do you have a favorite piece of clothing? And what secret lies behind it?

A short-sleeved T-shirt with V cutout – no secret, just my favorite piece of clothing.

Describe your favorite design object.

This applies to any design where I can see, just by looking at it, what problems came up during conception and realization, and how they were solved.

Why should designers also be visionaries and create utopias?

Utopias release certain energies which can stimulate a designer to push ahead. After all, what one wants to achieve as a goal is always ahead, not behind one.

How do you go about realizing your design concepts?

I struggle through the fights I'm subjected to in the phase of initial creation.

Does a design ever reach perfection?

Yes, for a while.

Why will a designer never create something which is based exclusively on a beautiful form?

A beautiful form all by itself can be a pleasure only to the eye – a concept and a significance, on the other hand, please the soul.

What does elegance have to do with simplicity?

Elegance has its origins in the human soul, which is light-hearted and simple.

Do you, as a designer, find it difficult to work for a company and create objects which carry your personal touch and style?

As I've already said: designing is a problem-solving process. The question here is merely another problem that's waiting to be solved.

BECAUSE FASHION APPEARS AND
GIVES THE MOMENT ITS VALID FORM, IT
ALREADY BELONGS TO YESTERDAY, TO
WHAT IS OLD AND WHAT HAS PASSED. […]
THE MOMENT NEGATES TIME AND
DURATION; IT ERASES THE TRACES OF
TIME, MAKING ITSELF ABSOLUTE, SELF-
EVIDENT, AND WITHOUT BLEMISH, THE
PERFECT MOMENT AS A REFLECTION
OF ETERNITY.
BARBARA VINKEN

FASHION AND PHOTOGRAPHY
THE INDIVIDUAL PERSPECTIVE
OF THE PHOTOGRAPHER

An interview with Peter Prix

What, in your opinion, makes a good fashion photographer?

To be convincing, photographers should have a good feel for the task in hand, must plan the images in their mind's eye in advance, and be intuitive during a photo shoot.

How did you get involved in fashion photography?

My fascination with photography began when I was six. Back then, I used my bike, a puddle or a tree as motifs. Later, in my school photography club, my classmates were my first models for fashion features in the school magazine. In my professional life, fashion photography has always been my main concern.

Are fashion photographers themselves subject to fashions?

Of course, fashion photographers live from trends, but they should retain their own hallmark.

Why should fashion support the person, rather than the other way round?

"Clothes make people" – to put it simply. There's nothing better than to create a self-confident, tasteful appearance through one's own style, supported by the latest fashion.

Why is style all about refinement and individualism?

The diversity within fashion should provide ample opportunity to dress tastefully. Unfortunately, not everyone has refined taste.

What line must a fashion photographer never cross?

Fashion photos should be imaginative and stimulating, but never tasteless.

What is the impetus behind your work with the Norintra design center?

As a freelance fashion photographer I met Annett Koeman, director of the Norintra design center, a few years ago. Our work together has always been very creative. When she called me about the Norintra "eveningwear" project, I jumped at the chance. Straight after the call my wife and I began to plan the shoot.

Why does a collection need to be captured in staged photographs in order to reach an audience?

People are inundated with images. You can reach the viewer only with staged and unusual photos.

Can you describe Norintra's eveningwear collection in just a few words?

The whole photography team was really excited by Norintra's eveningwear collection. Each individual piece is a perfect masterpiece by designer Angel Wong. Ready for the international catwalks. Fantastic!

What do closeness and distance mean for you? When do you feel people are getting too close and have overstepped the line?

For me, closeness is absolute understanding, sensing, and feeling without words. Distance makes me feel left out, leaves me cold.

What kind of photographs do you find particularly attractive?

All photographs that stimulate my imagination.

When, in your opinion, is fashion photography inspired?

Whenever all those involved are able to put all their feeling into it.

Wim Wenders, talking about Peter Lindbergh, said that a photographer's soul shows itself in each of his pictures. Do you agree?

I couldn't put it better myself.

Fashion designer Helmut Lang has described studios as such as a "window into the soul of artistic compulsion, resolve, and self-doubt." How would you describe your studio? What's the story behind it?

The studio gives me the space to create the photograph with light and artistic resources. The atmosphere of the studio is transferred to the image.

Does fashion photography turn the subject into the object?

You could say that. I always try to merge the external with the internal in order to create an object of desire.

What makes a good motif?

A good motif can come from anywhere. A wood, a landscape, a person – anything. It all comes down to the photographer's individual perspective.
What is the most fascinating thing about eveningwear? The material symbiosis of emotion and passion?

Eveningwear is the epitome of self-adornment. A low-cut or backless dress, both pay passionate tribute to a special evening. It's different from a skimpy bikini; the material of the dress covers up and at the same time reveals elsewhere a view of erotic forms. Combined with the numerous details of the dress and the elegance of movement, the overall result is a harmony that is indescribable.

FOR ME, DESIGN DOES NOT MEAN
REINVENTING THINGS, BUT REPLACING
BEAUTY OR UGLINESS WITH GOODNESS.
PHILIPPE STARCK

DESIGN OR NON-EXISTENCE
DESIGNERS PLAY A LEADING ROLE
IN SHAPING OUR FUTURE

An interview with Peter Zec

What conditions have to be fulfilled for a company's image to be perceived as a positive social asset?

A company can be viewed as an operationally closed system that differs from other systems through the form of its communication and the perception of its outer form. Thus the decisive factors in determining a company's image are the perception of that image or identity and the interpretations put upon its corporate statements. The more credible its image and communications, the more positively that image will be experienced as one of the company's social assets. Ultimately, however, it is always observers who take the decisions and make the assessments.

Can you comment on this quote from Otl Aicher: "Besides hard economic facts and figures, design is the very essence of a company."

Here, again, I would like to cite Otl Aicher, because he himself explained, very concisely and very pithily, the immense significance of design for corporate culture. In his writings, Aicher asserts that a company's founding idea, its internal actions, attitudes and structure, and its external manifestations in its products, corporate communications, and marketing have an inner coherence: "Design brings a company's technical and economic philosophy into the picture: its image, its identity simultaneously becomes its character and defines its mentality." And: "For a company, design is a life process whose purpose is to give intentions a concrete, tangible form. It turns wishes and desires into visible, observable phenomena." Design thus gives form not only to products, but also to ideas and to corporate philosophy, in other words to the company itself in its many facets. It "translates" intangible values, as it were, so that they can be experienced and perceived. Good design can, moreover, take such values on to an emotional level, thereby eliminating the need to use terms such as "tradition," "integrity" and the like.

What are the reasons for the increasing importance of design "as a formative cultural factor in society"? And why is design an essential criterion for product success in the global marketplace?

The reasons for the growing importance of design have their roots in the globalization of markets. In principle, everyone in the world can access the same knowledge resources, services, and products. The supply of goods and choice of services is, consequently, enormous and competition among companies for market share has intensified considerably. As a result, having scrambled in recent years to secure the best technical innovations, companies are now increasingly focusing on sophisticated design tailored to particular target groups in order to compete. Customer needs are therefore coming more and more to the fore as companies search

for the ideal form for a product. Even in less typical design areas such as life science design – that is, medical products, devices, and aids – a lot is happening. Prostheses and wheelchairs are becoming sporty, medical examination equipment is becoming less forbidding and more patient-friendly, and design is becoming altogether more sensitive, with consideration being given to emotional aspects as well as to the provision of innovative answers to difficult technical challenges. Nowadays almost nothing is possible without a qualitatively very high-grade design. As a result, design quality has increased continuously – not just at the top end but ultimately throughout the entire market. Of course this leads to more intense competition and means that companies in future will have to be even more innovative and use design to obtain long-term customer loyalty. It also means that it is important to respond to people's culturally determined demands, needs, fears, hopes, and wishes. It is essential in product development to take into account the cultural characteristics of different countries and markets without totally abandoning your own cultural identity.

Why is design always accompanied by the "risk of failure"?

The difficulty with design is that a universally applicable decision on what is good or bad design is simply not possible. And even when many people consider a certain shape or a particular creative style to be beautiful, this does not mean that the corresponding product is something they absolutely must have for themselves, so market success is particularly difficult to predict. Design is a matter of taste, which makes it inherently impossible to objectify the design decision. Nevertheless, there have been attempts at objectification, such as that made by architect Louis H. Sullivan based on the dictum "form follows function." However, even with this so-called "functionalism," we are dealing only with a particular style of design and not an inviolable design truth.

If a valid objectification is at all possible it can achieved only if a multitude of people agree to attribute the same meaning to a design object. This decision-making process is based primarily not on ideas or opinions, but rather on communication. Furthermore, design competitions make a type of objectification possible when design decisions are being made. True, every juror's decision is a subjective judgment, but in competitions there are always several jurors with high levels of expertise making simultaneous decisions on a product, which lead ultimately to that product being commended or rejected. One can therefore rely on an expert judgment. However, all other decision makers are of course free to accept this judgment or to make a different decision for them-

selves. Against such a background, it is not difficult to understand that design always runs the risk of rejection.

What differentiates a designer from an artist?

To return once again to the words of Otl Aicher: "Design renounces the aesthetic absolutism of art and seeks the aesthetics of use." In other words, one can say that an artist is not beholden to anybody with his creations. He is totally autonomous and free to work as he sees fit. He can, therefore, in the truest sense of the word do what he wants without having to take others into consideration, as long as he does not violate the rights of others.

With design, the situation is wholly different. As a rule, a designer always needs a customer, for whom he provides a service. At the same time, it is crucial to the success of any design exercise that designer and customer have similar perceptions of the task in hand and that they work together with mutual respect and trust.

Why does creativity require freedom?

The contribution of designers to the shaping of our living and working environments cannot be overestimated. Design has played just as great a role as technology in shaping the material world over the last 85 years. While technology has produced new ideas, new materials, and new systems, it is design and architecture that have made these discoveries understandable and acceptable and advanced them through communication. Designers thus play a leading role in shaping our future. They take a look at the world, how it is, and imagine how it might be developed further. Basically, today – from a technical point of view – almost anything is possible. All that is lacking is ideas for visionary applications of new technologies. This is why it is so important that creators be allowed the freedom to think without constraint, to try things out, to take a look around. This is the only way really new things can come about.

All their creativity notwithstanding, however, designers are generally very much in thrall to the power of the factual in their daily work. They are constantly in dialog with customers, marketing people or engineers and have to reduce the most varied specifications, expectations, and product requirements to a common denominator during the design process.

The tyranny of reality is, however, the greatest enemy of creativity. Rules and general conditions that are too tightly drawn do not leave sufficient room for creativity. Time and again, companies design their products according to strict guidelines in order to avoid possible risks. This cannot guarantee success in the long term, however. In the ultimately irresolvable tension between what is conceivable and what is possible within the limits set by the customer or by reality, the aim must be to achieve the best that is possible and to always be pushing the boundaries a little further back. Only those who are able to develop something new themselves will never have to be content with copying the developments of others. They are much more interested in competing with the best in the market and fighting for market leadership.

Why is design an integral element of a company's strategic action plan that transcends pure product design?

For more than ten years now I've been observing and analyzing companies whose success is based essentially on the continuous pursuit of an innovative design policy. In that time, I've been able consistently to identify seven attributes that characterize successful, design-oriented companies and at the same time differentiate them from less successful competitors.

To be successful with design does not mean concentrating on one product or one segment of the product range. However good and successful they may be in their own right, individual products count for little when it comes to securing a company's success. Design has to be viewed and implemented as an integral part of a company's overall management strategy. It is also true that a struggling business cannot recover solely through design. In fact, the reverse is true with design, true to the Latin phrase "Mens sana in corpore sano." Successfully managed companies can either become more successful through design or at least safeguard their success in the long term. The best way to ensure this is a corporate management strategy that is both innovation and design-oriented.

Reduced to its essential elements, the exceptional performance of all successful design-oriented companies is characterized by the following seven attributes: the primacy of quality, the will to create, an awareness of value, the willingness to communicate, scope for creativity, the courage to experiment, and an understanding of the customer.

What characterizes products that are particularly successful in the market?

Successful products differ from less successful ones in being able to establish themselves in the real world. There have been many different attempts to define good design and establish rules and guidelines by which designs can be categorized and rated.

"Design thus gives form not only to products, but also to ideas and to corporate philosophy, in other words to the company itself in its many facets. It 'translates' intangible values, as it were, so that they can be experienced and perceived."

The beauty of function,
the beauty of seductiveness,
the beauty of use,
the beauty of responsibility.

Ultimately, however, what characterizes good design is that it is successful. The reality in which this success takes place can be divided into four phases, which occur at different times in a product's life cycle. These various stages in a product's life cycle can also be compared to the life course of an individual who, over time, goes through various stages of beauty, from childhood through adolescence to maturity and finally to old age. Similarly, in the case of a product personality, we can speak of the four "beauties of design" that an object has to acquire in the course of its life cycle in order to be completely successful. The necessary conditions for this must be put in place in the product development phase. The four beauties are:

the beauty of function,
the beauty of seductiveness,
the beauty of use,
the beauty of responsibility.

In the case of the beauty of function, the aim is to fit a product's form to its purpose. During this phase, which takes place at the beginning of the product development cycle, designers and manufacturers investigate how a particular purpose can become an object and in what shapes, colors, and materials. Not only does form follow function, which is usually technically defined, but it must also meet the expectations of users.

The beauty of seductiveness has to play a role alongside these formal design aspects. By this I mean a characteristic or element that is largely unrelated to a product's use but is intended rather to seduce and give pleasure. Seductiveness is meant here in the best sense of the word, to denote a love of the product and not, for instance, the superficial manipulation of consumers through advertising and marketing activities.

The beauty of use may at first glance appear to be closely linked with the beauty of function described above; however, it means something different. There are things that function superbly in themselves but are not at all user-friendly, for example, all those high-tech devices that can do everything, but which we are barely able to operate in such a way as to make all their functions accessible to the user. The more easily a product can be operated – that means used – the greater its utility for the user.

Finally, the beauty of responsibility is playing an ever-growing role in product aesthetics and market success. What is meant by responsibility here is, above all, a product's environmental sustainability. In my opinion these are the priorities a product must fulfill in order to be particularly successful.

Why is it that in the fashion industry high-quality strategies can lead to better, more sustained differentiation than is possible by offering mass-produced goods at considerably lower prices?

I wouldn't necessarily concur with such a sweeping statement. Don't forget that that the two strategies are aimed at different target groups and have different objectives and both are therefore perfectly valid. Nevertheless, I recommend what I believe is the more sustainable path to differentiation through quality, from both a personal and a business point of view. Fashion is indeed a fast-moving business; customers, however, are much better off in the medium term if they don't chase trends at any price but opt rather for higher-quality products that are timeless and last for years. That way they can, over time, build up an extensive, high-quality wardrobe, which can always be updated with a few fashionable items.

In recent years, consumer behavior of this kind, which anyone with a healthy dose of common sense would subscribe to anyway, has been further reinforced by increased environmental awareness among the wider public. As a result of recent dire predictions of the catastrophic consequences of global warming, food scandals, and so on, a new attitude towards consumption has emerged that runs counter to the "stinginess is cool" mentality. Regional products, organic foods, furniture that satisfies people's desire for wood and other materials to be used more responsibly – these things are all more sought-after than ever and consumers are prepared to pay an appropriate price in exchange for quality and fair trade. What is at stake here is, above all, trust: in manufacturers and their products, in socially acceptable business practices, even if manufacturing has to take place in low-wage countries, and in responsible behavior toward people and resources. A "responsible society" is emerging and as a result endowing products with meaning is becoming a way for companies to gain a competitive advantage – regardless of whether they are operating in the food, furniture, energy or fashion industry.

What will be the key issues facing environmental planning and product design in future?

Designers have one of their most important roles to play wherever they are involved in the care, planning, and shaping of our environment, since the way we order our world impacts on our cultural identity perhaps even more than our interaction with industrially manufactured goods. That is to say, the layout of streets, squares, and buildings as well as of residential and business districts exercises a considerable influence on our quality of life. In no other area of life do human beings and the artificial surroundings they create encroach upon the natural world to such a great extent as they do in urban spaces. Thus it is all the more important that our activities be based on a heightened awareness of our responsibility towards the natural world and the environment. At the same time, ecological concerns and environmentally-friendly practices are becoming increasingly important in design. In both environmental planning and product design, ever greater efforts will have to be made in future to economize on resources and to reduce waste as much as possible in order to avoid the problems associated with waste disposal. In order to achieve these objectives, designers must, wherever possible, be constantly operating at the forefront of technical innovation in the area of new raw materials and manufacturing processes.

What does the term "sustainable design" mean to you?

"Sustainable design" does indeed sound rather dry and boring, but for me it has thoroughly positive connotations. I particularly like the way that just by itself the phrase makes clear the far-reaching influence that design has on such important areas of our lives as environmental protection and energy consumption. Design is not just a matter of additional styling but is a significant influencing factor on many of the important decisions that have to be taken at a very early stage in the product development process.

Sustainable design is therefore about designing products, services, public spaces, buildings, streets – in short, our environment – in such a way that the use of non-renewable energies and raw materials is reduced and damage to the environment minimized.

Why is fashion an important seismograph for identifying general design trends? And when is it genuinely convincing?

The reason is that the fashion industry moves faster than virtually any other area of design. A new collection has to be presented at least twice a year, and sometimes the designs are completed just weeks before they go into production. Thus the fashion industry has to react quickly and keep a very close eye on exactly what is happening on the scene as well as in other countries and continents, on which artists are currently on the up, and on what is going on in Internet forums – in order to detect the smallest changes of mood or sentiment in society and thus anticipate incipient trends to which designers in other areas can react only very much more slowly.

What does a design center such as Norintra in Hong Kong have to do to make itself stand out from the competition?

In order to set yourself apart from competitors you have to be different. This applies to a company's inner as well as its outer form. Absolutely the only way to achieve the necessary differentiation is repeatedly to take decisions that differ from those of others. This requires considerable self-confidence. It is necessary, therefore, to set new yardsticks and standards that can also be clearly perceived as such. In doing so, you have repeatedly to summon up the courage to think and act differently in order to be able to push back boundaries. However, there's no point in being different at all costs just in order to be different. Each attempt at differentiation must also always be associated with a specific new quality. You must always act in a way that increases the number of possibilities. In this way you're always creating opportunities to break away from the beaten path, to look afresh at your own practices, and to adapt to new circumstances.

"Appearances matter." To what extent does this old saying, which you often cite, also apply to the market presence of a design center such as Norintra?

The importance of a company's corporate design in shaping outsiders' perceptions cannot be underestimated. This applies particularly to a design center that is on the verge of making its first major appearance before the public. Alongside the collection that will be presented on that occasion, Norintra also has to position itself correctly right from the outset. In plain language that means that everything – starting with the premises in which the creative staff work, the choice of location for the first presentation, the information brochures for the umbrella brand name right down to the logo for each individual sub-label – must convey the core values of creativity, attitude, and lifestyle as well as social responsibility. With strong brands this is all of a piece – and the brand itself is not a company asset for nothing.

The head of our design center, Annett Koeman, is of the opinion that good design and a social conscience make a wonderful combination. This is why the mixture of fair trade and a sense of style plays an important role in her design center. Do you share her view?

Of course. There is nothing more desirable than finding beauty, functionality, quality of use, and social responsibility combined in a product and then also being able to afford it.

"There is nothing more desirable than finding beauty, functionality, quality of use, and social responsibility combined in a product and then also being able to afford it."

PEOPLE NEED GRACE IN THEIR MOVE-
MENTS AND BEHAVIOR, BECAUSE GRACE
IS A SYNONYM FOR GOOD TASTE, FRIEND-
LINESS, BALANCE, AND HARMONY.
PAULO COELHO

ABOUT THE AUTHORS

Dr. Thomas Middelhoff

was born in Düsseldorf and studied Business Studies in Münster. After completing a PhD in 1986, he held different positions at Bertelsmann AG, including those of Managing Director of Elsnerdruck GmbH and Mohndruck GmbH, and Chairman of the Supervisory Board from 1998 to 2002. From 2003 to 2005 Middelhoff was Head of Europe of the corporate investment company Investcorp International Ltd., London. Since 2005 he has been Chief Executive Officer of KarstadtQuelle AG in Essen, which has been trading under the name of Arcandor AG since July 2007. Middelhoff is a member of several supervisory boards. He is, among other positions, Chairman of the Supervisory Board of Thomas Cook, moneybookers.com, Senator Entertainment, and Polestar, as well as member of the Supervisory Board of The New York Times. He is actively involved in the advancement of corporate governance in Germany, demanding a marked increase in professionalism in this area. Since May 2006 he has been a supporter and member of the Advisory Board of the Institute for Corporate Governance (ICG) at the University Witten/Herdecke. For more information visit: www.arcandor.com

Annett Koeman

is Director of Norintra Ltd., Hong Kong. She began her career as Product Manager at Levi Strauss Germany in 1988, but her professional life soon focused on the Far East, where she held management positions at Seidensticker Hong Kong, Hugo Boss Far East, Otto International Hong Kong, and Together Ltd., which is part of the Otto Group. She has been head of the Norintra design center in Hong Kong since March 2007. For more information visit: www.norintra.com

Dr. Emmanuel Siregar

was appointed Member of the Board of Directors of Karstadt Warenhaus GmbH in June 2007. He is in charge of Human Resources and Organization and is also Labor Director of Karstadt Warenhaus GmbH. After obtaining a PhD in 1994, having previously completed a degree in Theology, he began his corporate career first as a trainer and consultant. From 1996 to 1997 Siregar worked as a management consultant and trainer for the Gesellschaft für Kommunikation und Weiterbildung, Hamburg. The Brussels-born son of Japanese and Indonesian parents then joined Fielmann AG, Hamburg. After becoming Departmental Manager for Human Resources in 2002, he was appointed Divisional Director of Human Resources and Human Resources Development as well as Labor Director of Fielmann AG in 2004. He held this position until he joined Karstadt Warenhaus GmbH. For more information visit: www.karstadt.de

Dr. Alexandra Hildebrandt

has been Head of Communication Social Affairs at Arcandor AG (previously KarstadtQuelle AG) since 2006. She studied Literary Theory, Psychology, and Book Studies before managing the internal communication of an international building materials company from 2000 to 2005. Alexandra Hildebrandt is the author of several non-fiction books and writes for radio and television. Her most recent book, "Die Spur des Grenzgängers. Leben als Passion," was published by Junfermann in 2006. For more information visit: www.arcandor.com

Peter Prix

was assistant to Willi Moegle in the field of product and advertising photography in Stuttgart-Leinfelden from 1972 to 1973. From 1978 to 1994 Peter Prix worked as a freelance photographer in Karlsruhe, specializing in fashion (for national and international clients). In December 1994 the company was sold to its employees. Since 1995 Prix has worked as a freelance photographer specializing in high-quality photography and exhibitions. In 2001 he received the Kodak Calendar Prize for the "Algarve" golf calendar in the "GREEN edition" team. He has taken part in several exhibitions. For more information visit: www.prix-photography.de

Prof. Dr. Peter Zec

is President of the Design Zentrum Nordrhein Westfalen in Essen, Germany, and initiator of the red dot design award, one of the most prestigious international prizes for product and communication design. In 1993 he accepted a professorship of Business Communication at the University of Applied Sciences Berlin. In 2005 he became President of Icsid (International Council of Societies of Industrial Design), the international umbrella organization of design in Montreal, Canada. As an expert on the German as well as the international design scene, he is the editor of numerous design books, among them the red dot design yearbook. In October 2006 the leading German magazine for economics, WirtschaftsWoche, named Peter Zec one of "20 creative, unconventional thinkers who have changed the appearance of their companies and created completely new markets." For more information visit: www.red-dot.de

IMPRINT

Picture credits

Norintra eveningwear
Photos: Peter Prix (Copyright: Norintra)
Coverfoto, 7, 13, 17, 25, 35, 41, 52, 64, 74,
92-105, 107, 111, 113, 123

Norintra House of Fashion
Photos: Rainer Kwiotek, Zeitenspiegel, Stuttgart
(Copyright: Arcandor AG)
14, 21, 22, 27, 30, 32, 44, 49, 51, 63, 67, 70,
73, 81, 82, 86, 89, 90

Marietta Slomka and Angel Wong Pui Shan
Photo: Frank Schultze, Zeitenspiegel, Stuttgart
(Copyright: Arcandor AG)
58

Norintra designers
Photos: private
43, 55, 61, 69, 77, 85

Norintra "Cube"
Kontext Kommunikation, Heidelberg
38

Alexandra Hildebrandt
Photo: Annett Bourquin, Berlin
(Copyright: Arcandor AG)
37

Thomas Middelhoff
Photo: Arcandor AG
9

Peter Prix
Photo: A. Biber
109

Emmanuel Siregar
Photo: Arcandor AG
19

Peter Zec
Photo: Michael Dannenmann, Düsseldorf
115

Bibliographic information published by the Deutsche Nationalbibliothek. The Deutsche Nationalbibliothek lists this publication in
the Deutsche Nationalbibliografie; detailed bibliographic data are
available on the Internet at http://dnb.d-nb.de.

ISBN: 978-3-89939-094-0
© 2007 red dot edition, Essen

Printed in Germany

Publisher
red dot edition, Gelsenkirchener Str. 181, 45309 Essen
T +49 (0)201 81 41 822, F +49 (0)201 81 41 810
info@red-dot.de, www.red-dot.de

Worldwide distribution
avedition GmbH, Königsallee 57, 71638 Ludwigsburg
T +49 (0)7141 14 77 391, F +49 (0)7141 14 77 399
kontakt@avedition.de, www.avedition.de

reddot **edition**

Edited by
Helmut Merkel, Alexandra Hildebrandt, and Annett Koeman

Interviews and quotations
Alexandra Hildebrandt

Project supervision
Elmar Schüller

Project management
Sabine Wöll, Sabine Meier

Editorial work
Astrid Ruta

Proofreading
Klaus Dimmler, Essen
Danko Szabó, Gräfelfing

Translation
Jan Stachel-Williamson, Christchurch
Bruce Stout, Grafenau
the translators ag, Heidelberg
Andreas Zantop, Berlin
Christiane Zschunke, Frankfurt/Main

Design and layout
Markwald & Neusitzer, Frankfurt/Main

Production, lithography and printing
printmediapart GmbH & Co. KG, Gelsenkirchen

LIST OF PUBLICATIONS
NORINTRA (SELECTION)

Anja Ruf: Verantwortung ist sexy. Moralischer Konsum wird in der Modebranche zum Wettbewerbsfaktor.
In: einsEntwicklungspolitik, no. 13/14 (2007), p. 19

Arne Philipp Klug: Nachhaltiges Modedesign aus Fernost.
In: global21. Magazin für nachhaltiges Investment, no. 3 (August 2007), p. 38 f.
Also at: www.macondo.de (as of September 3, 2007)

Kulturelle Vielfalt. A publication by Arcandor AG.
Hong Kong design center.
In cooperation with Culture Counts. Essen, Hong Kong (self-published) 2007
Also at: www.culturecounts.de (as of September 3, 2007)

Gutes Design und soziales Gewissen. Kulturelle Vielfalt als Wettbewerbsfaktor in der Globalisierung.
In: Kommunikation & Seminar, no. 4 (2007), p. 49

Best Practice-Beispiel: Norintra House of Fashion.
In: Jahrbuch Kulturmarken (Causales, Berlin 2007), p. 138 f.

(about Angel Wong, Norintra)
Arcandor unterstützt Deutschen Kulturförderpreis in Berlin.
In: www.nachhaltigwirtschaften.net (as of September 2, 2007)

(about Angel Wong, Norintra)
Weil es Spaß macht. Warum engagiert sich die Wirtschaft für die Kunst? Erklärungen bei der Verleihung des 2. Deutschen Kulturförderpreises.
In: Süddeutsche Zeitung (September 8, 2007)

Norintra. Gesucht – der Name der Roben.
In: maz. Zeitung für Mitarbeiter des Arcandor Konzerns (September 2007), p. 3

(about Annett Koeman)
WE WOMEN + ECONOMY. THE BOOK.
Volume 2/2008: Frauen der deutschen Wirtschaft.
Published by Anne Lehr, Munich 2008